The Transformation of America

As Government Grows Liberty Yields

George E Pfautsch

authorHOUSE®

AuthorHouse™
1663 Liberty Drive
Bloomington, IN 47403
www.authorhouse.com
Phone: 1-800-839-8640

Published by AuthorHouse 2/8/2013

ISBN: 978-1-4817-1273-6 (sc)
ISBN: 978-1-4817-1287-3 (e)

Library of Congress Control Number: 2013901895

OTHER BOOKS
BY
GEORGE E PFAUTSCH

Redefining Morality
A Threat to our Nation

Times of Greatness
Morality Matters

Flawed Justice
When our Unalienable Rights are Ignored

The Purpose of Life
Know Him, Love Him, Serve Him

The Wisdom of our Soul

A Case of Modern Day Pharisees
The Need for Holiness

Hey Kids, Want Some Chocolates?
My Family's Journey to Freedom
(co-authored with Melitta Strandberg)

A Man From Two Worlds
(co-authored with Leroy New)

Contents

Preface

This book was begun more than four years ago, shortly after President Barack Obama's Administration had been sworn into office for its first term. At that time the nation was in a "Great Recession". President Obama was touting the need for a new health care plan and was also promoting a huge stimulus package in an attempt to minimize the results of the Great Recession.

At that time it was my decision not to publish the book, because it appeared that the aforementioned plans of the Obama Administration would have a significant impact on the economic situation of our country and on what I had written about the economy.

Another factor contributed to my decision. Most of my books have addressed a form of morality, which I describe as a faith-based morality. It was and is my belief that such a morality was the "national morality" foreseen by the founding fathers of this nation. It was my concern that this book would be seen more as a political writing and not as a writing on morality and that is not my intent. Both major political parties have been instrumental in shaping the morality of our nation.

Government plays a major role in our lives and in determining the morality of a nation. But the people of a nation also play a major role. They vote and by their voting indicate their preference for the type of government they desire; or at least for the candidates and issues they favor or disfavor.

A fairly significant issue of this book relates to the economy of this nation. It is my view that to a fairly large degree the economy of a nation is shaped by the culture and morality of a nation.

In recent months, it has been my decision to proceed with the publication of this book. Because of the events of the last four years some figures needed updating, but generally my views required very little updating due to the lapse in time.

In most ways, the decisions made by our government in the past four years, if anything, have had a slightly more negative impact on my outlook than stated in my original draft. The nation's debt is somewhat greater than earlier projected, federal tax increases are being considered, and the involvement of the Federal Reserve has also been somewhat more adverse, which is largely due to the additional debt incurred.

It has not only been the last four years that have contributed to the economic transformation of our nation. It has been a gradual but steady transformation, which has accelerated in the past few years. The transformation of our national faith-based morality has also been a gradual transformation. In the process of transformation, our freedoms have diminished.

George E Pfautsch

Introduction

"The care of human life and happiness, and not their destruction, is the first and only legitimate object of good government". Our third president, Thomas Jefferson, made that observation about the role of government. Freedom has been an important right for the care of human life and happiness throughout the life of our country. However, as countries grow and change, so does the concept of freedom.

Jefferson also noted that, "The course of history shows that as government grows, liberty decreases".

History most assuredly provides us the lesson that the evolution of things is a normal process of life on earth. In this nation many things have changed since 1776. The examination of such transformation on "the care of human life and happiness" is the purpose of this book.

On September 11, 2001 terrorists attacked this nation. The terrorists seized planes from United States airlines to fly into both of the World Trade Center buildings in New York. The two buildings collapsed shortly thereafter and many died. On the same day the coordinated efforts of the terrorists resulted in another plane destroying a part of the Pentagon in Washington, D.C., killing hundreds more. A fourth plane hijacked by terrorists crashed in western Pennsylvania after the bravery of passengers, all of whom were also killed, prevented the terrorists from flying into another unknown site. Their bravery undoubtedly saved the lives of others who were the unknown targets. The after-effects of these terrorists' acts are still with us in the form of increased and enhanced security measures.

As we move through the second decade of the third millennium, our nation is slowly recovering from one of the worst, if not the worst, recessions since the Great Depression of the 1930's. A decline in the value of home prices caused many homeowners to default on mortgages. These defaults and other poor financial decisions began an erosion in the creditworthiness of financial institutions, which in turn caused a credit crisis in the country. Government intervention by means of unprecedented bailouts of financial institutions and other corporations together with massive stimulus packages did not prevent economic difficulties for all aspects of the nation's economy.

The two above events have had a significant effect on the lives of many of the people in this country. They have accelerated the transformation of our nation and have further restricted the freedom of individuals via an ever increasing amount of federal regulations.

The attacks by terrorists have resulted in the aforementioned increased security measures and have led us into two wars in Afghanistan and Iraq. The national debt was substantially increased because of these wars. The effect of that did not help our economic difficulties.

With the recession that began in 2008 came even greater deficits and massive increases in the national debt. The decline in home values and the stock market have also had an impact on many Americans. Pension funds, 401-k funds and personal stock holdings declined and eroded the wealth of most of us. It will take years to recover those losses. The huge increases in interest expense required to service the national debt will have adverse effects on us, our children and grandchildren and probably future generations beyond our grandchildren.

The news media and other pundits analyze these events at great length. But, they are probably no better at forecasting the future impacts of these events than they were in forecasting the massive recession we have experienced. Recessions and recoveries have always been difficult to forecast and that is still the case.

It is my belief that while the above events undoubtedly have had major impacts on this nation's economic system, there have also been many other changes, which while being subtler, have also contributed to our economic difficulties. These changes have evolved over many years and not only contributed to changes in our economic system but also in our social and cultural values.

If our founding fathers were alive today, they would find an American economic and cultural system not anticipated by them. To the degree that such changes came about because of the growth of our society they are to be expected. Some amount of regulations and laws are necessary to maintain a better society. While that is true, it is far more debatable if the underlying values, which made for a great nation and that were understood by our forefathers needed to be changed but changed they have been. Some of the changes have been for the good but far too many of the economic and societal changes have impacted our nation in an adverse manner. It is not unreasonable to believe that societal values also have an effect on our economic system. That will be further explored in this book.

Many of the societal values of today would have shocked our founding fathers. The society of their era was rather puritanical whereas our current values have very elastic boundaries of morality. There are very few rules that today restrict in any meaningful way the moral conduct of people. Almost any type of behavior becomes adjudicated as a human right of one type or another without any implications of what such judgments may have on a society. The general welfare of the nation gets ignored in the process.

Human beings are flawed and those flaws without limitations imposed by a society have an impact on the society. They also subject that society to change. Ultimately they impact on the well-being of all society, including the economic system.

In this book we will examine how the societal, moral, and economic changes that have taken place over the course of our country's history have transformed this nation, not only economically but culturally as well. The impact of such transformation on individual freedoms will also be examined.

We will first examine the impacts of events that have caused economic changes and then look at changes in our value system. Finally we will review how these changes have transformed us into our society of today and how such changes are likely to impact us in future years.

Chapter 1 --- Our Social and Economic Foundation

Our forefathers established some broad moral principles when they established this nation. I refer to those moral principles as a faith-based morality. A faith-based morality simply acknowledges a supernatural Creator, who provides humans with certain inalienable rights and creates all humans as equals in His eyes. Such a morality is not partial to or attributable to any specific religion but recognizes that a higher form of morality is necessary, and which cannot be provided by a purely secular morality.

Our founding fathers understood that a faith-based morality was necessary in order to protect and benefit all citizens. This nation was founded on that belief. Nothing could make that more clear than the reasons they noted in the preamble of the Declaration of Independence.

When in the course of human events, it becomes necessary for one people to dissolve the political bands which have connected them with another, and to assume among the powers of the earth, the separate and equal station to which the Laws of Nature and Nature's God entitle them, a decent respect to the opinions of mankind requires that they should declare the causes which impel them to separation.

<u>We hold these truths to be self-evident, that all men are created equal, that they are endowed by their Creator with certain unalienable Rights, that among these are Life, Liberty and the pursuit of Happiness.</u> (underlining added for emphasis)

That to secure these rights, governments are instituted among men, deriving their just powers from the consent of the governed, – that whenever any form of government becomes destructive of these ends, it is the right of the people to alter or abolish it…

No words ever written can better express the rights of citizens and that the purpose of government is to help its citizens achieve such rights.

Some years later the founding fathers enacted the Constitution that incorporated the principles contained in the Declaration.

We the People of the United States, in Order to form a more perfect Union, establish Justice, insure domestic tranquility, provide for the common defence, promote the General

Welfare, and secure the Blessings of Liberty to ourselves and our Posterity, do ordain and establish this Constitution for the United States of America.

These preambles to the Declaration and the Constitution established the broad principles that a government should follow if it wished to exist. When these principles are not followed then government loses its right to exist. The rest of the Constitution set forth the rights of citizens. Such rights were always intended to support the broad principles first set forth in the Declaration and the Preamble to the Constitution. Too often these principles have been forgotten in determining how the rights of citizens should be adjudicated.

Many of our founding fathers, who signed the Declaration also signed the Constitution. Some who signed one document were unable to sign the other because other important duties required their presence elsewhere. But as a group of leaders they were in full support of both documents.

Among those leaders, several were in the forefront of laying the foundation of governance for this nation. They included our first four presidents - Washington, Adams, Jefferson and Madison. Two others, Benjamin Franklin and Alexander Hamilton, were also instrumental in laying the foundation for the best government ever conceived by humans. Their collective genius included

3

the recognition that human beings are flawed and tend to be corrupted by power. They believed that too much power in the hands of those who govern was inherently bad. They recognized the necessity to segregate powers at the highest level of government. They also recognized that certain inalienable rights are granted by a higher and righteous power. When these rights are observed we are a great and good nation. When not observed we are something less.

Of the six men noted above, three were on the committee of five men who were appointed to draft the Declaration - Jefferson, Adams and Franklin. It was Jefferson, who prepared the first draft, which he sent to Adams and Franklin for their input. Obviously these men agreed on the existence of the "self-evident" truths, as did many leaders in this country at that time. Madison would play an important role in the drafting of the Constitution and Hamilton would be instrumental in matters pertaining to the financial system of the country.

When society and government acknowledge the inalienable rights and ensure the equality of citizens, we observe a faith-based morality. Our first president noted the importance of such a morality when he left office. In his farewell address to the nation he noted that morality was the springboard to popular government. He also stated that, "Reason and experience forbid us to expect that national morality can prevail in exclusion of religious principle" (faith-based morality).

Benjamin Franklin basically stated the same thoughts when he said, "True religion and good morals are the only solid foundations of public liberty and happiness. Only a virtuous people are capable of freedom. As nations become more corrupt and vicious, they have more need of a master"(bigger government). Future events in this nation would prove his words to be very true.

If the inalienable right of freedom should be afforded to human beings, should it not also be afforded to other aspects of a society? It seems to logically follow that if a government understands the importance of the inalienable right to freedom for individuals, a free enterprise system for the economy would also be the best form of an economic system. It is the capitalistic or free enterprise system, which best incorporates the recognition of the inalienable rights of humans. Nevertheless, the flawed actions of free human beings and a free enterprise system require laws and regulations (masters) to prevent abuses.

Hamilton, as Secretary of the Treasury under Washington, would be the primary proponent of a national bank, which helped bring financial stability to a fledgling nation. However, this country in its early days was a largely agrarian nation and a sophisticated economic system was not yet a necessity, but nothing in the founding fathers' ideals for this new country stood in the way of a free enterprise system.

In addition to the inalienable rights of life and liberty for all citizens of this country, which have helped all people pursue happiness, we also began with an economic system that would make it possible for its citizens to thrive economically. The foundations for a free and prosperous people were indeed laid by the founding fathers of this nation. For the next few chapters of this book we will examine the growth of this nation's economic system and how it meshed with the social values of the nation and how it led to prosperity.

But we will not stop with just viewing the progress of this nation's social and economic system. In recent years this nation has slowly but surely changed, to some degree, the social and economic values established by the founding fathers. We will assess those changes. Those changes have had a transforming impact on this nation's value system. As noted earlier, rules and regulations are necessary to provide the proper oversight to a free system for citizens and their economy. As long as such changes continue to contain and incorporate the ideals of the founding fathers they are fine.

However, changes that begin departing from the

values foreseen by the founding fathers are not fine. Throughout our history, we have had situations that have not been in accord with those principles or values such as slavery, lack of rights for women, poor treatment of Native Americans and the internment of Japanese-Americans during World War II. Many of those violations of human rights have been corrected. They were corrected, because this nation ultimately recognized that all human beings are created equal and have the inalienable rights that can only be endowed by their Creator.

During the past fifty to sixty years, the changes in our value system have been more pronounced than during any other period in our history. A few of these changes have been for the good but some have proven to be a significant negative deviation from the national morality noted by our first president. The intent of this book is not only to note the most significant changes but to also look at the impact they have on this nation today and may have in the future.

Chapter 2 ~~~ Capitalism Versus Socialism

With the election of President Obama in 2008 the debate of capitalism versus socialism has been elevated in this country. Adding fuel to the debate is the deep recession that also began in 2008. The need or lack thereof for government to financially assist large financial institutions as well as other large corporations has legitimately raised the issue of the government's role in the economic system of this nation.

Before any meaningful debate on this subject is undertaken some definitions are useful. The first is to define capitalism. Adam Smith is often credited as being the father of capitalism. That is somewhat erroneous for a number of reasons. Smith, himself, never defined the economic system he advocated as capitalism in his book, "The Wealth of Nations". Smith was merely defining an economic system that he believed was better attuned to his time than "mercantilism". Even before Smith, the lassez-faire (hands off) view for an economic system had been promoted.

Smith was a moral philosopher and he did believe that a "free market" was the best way to produce the proper amount and variety of goods. He correctly believed that one who produces goods does so in his own self-interest and would produce only that which was needed by consumers. He referred to this belief as "the invisible hand". The invisible hand would produce what consumers wanted.

He put it simply as follows: "It is not from the benevolence of the butcher, the brewer, or the baker that we expect our dinner, but from their regard to their own interest. We address ourselves, not to their humanity but to their self-love and never talk to them of our own necessities but of their advantages". Smith believed that by doing this the producer was promoting the common good since it would be in the producer and consumer's interest to produce that which the consumer needed or wanted.

Smith was in fact promoting a free enterprise system and that may also be a better description of our economic system than the word capitalism. They are used interchangeably. The word capitalism is more correctly attributable to Karl Marx who used it to denigrate the free enterprise system.

Smith wrote "The Wealth of Nations" in 1776, which was the same year that this nation declared its independence. It is an interesting coincidence that this nation declared its independence at the same time that a moral philosopher was hailing the benefits of a free enterprise system.

The free enterprise system is very compatible with the reasons our founding fathers gave for establishing this nation. If our creator gives humans the inalienable right to freedom then it logically follows that free human beings should be permitted to follow a free economic or enterprise system.

The moral principle that says men deserve to be free also says that an economic system should be established by a nation that recognizes a free enterprise system. Whether one calls it a lassez-faire economic system, a free enterprise economic system or a capitalistic system, the important principle is that, regardless of what it is called, a free enterprise system is best suited for a nation that values a social system based on the moral principle that human beings have the inalienable right to freedom. The flaws of such an economic and social system are attributable to the flaws of humans, not the flaws of the system.

Nevertheless, it is wise and appropriate to recognize that flawed humans operate the free enterprise system and that the greed or excessive self-interests of humans can create flaws in a free system. Franklin properly noted that if and when a nation becomes corrupt it has the need of masters.

The person that probably had the greatest influence on advancing the need for government intervention in the free enterprise system was John Maynard Keynes, who was one of the world's foremost economists. Keynes believed that the modern capitalistic or free enterprise system did not always perform at top efficiency. He further believed that government needed to utilize monetary and fiscal policies to correct these inefficiencies and that such intervention was necessary to mitigate periods of economic depressions or economic booms. In our economic system today, Keynes' view can be satisfied largely by the current Federal Reserve System, as long as the federal government maintains a prudent fiscal budget. Keynes did not disavow the free enterprise system, but believed that an advanced free enterprise system needed occasional government intervention.

The problem with the theories advanced by Smith and Keynes is that they did not anticipate how much other government interventions such as taxation, laws and regulations could also impact the functioning of a free enterprise system. Such interventions by the government of this nation will be addressed in the next chapter.

The purpose of this chapter is to make a comparison of the capitalistic or free enterprise system with a system where economies are planned or determined by government. The latter systems come under the broad term of "socialism".

In summarizing the merits of the free enterprise or capitalistic economic system, it is important to remember that it is the system which best recognizes the inalienable right to freedom. If a country is founded on the belief that freedom is important to the national morality of a nation, then it needs to be recognized that the free enterprise system is a part of that important social fabric of a nation. It is also correct to believe that Adam Smith understood and properly proclaimed that a free enterprise system was the most efficient way of providing the goods and services for consumers. The free enterprise system therefore has two great advantages over any other system; i.e. the recognition of the inalienable right to freedom and also that it is the most efficient economic system.

Because humans are flawed it is also necessary to understand the shortcomings of a free enterprise system in an advanced economy. Karl Marx was somewhat correct when he noted that capitalism could be oppressive to its workers and citizens. The never-ending struggle and debate of a modern advanced capitalistic nation is how to best provide the oversight and intervention necessary to prevent the excesses of a totally free economic system. Dear Mr. Franklin, how much intervention must the master impose?

In this nation today, the government is being accused more and more of drifting toward socialism. It is therefore appropriate to examine socialism in more detail and understand its strengths and weaknesses.

To a large degree socialism found its roots due to the excesses of the free enterprise system. As the free enterprise system expanded into factories and others areas of mass production there was exploitation of workers. Workers were subjected to long working hours. Pay and working conditions were poor. Child labor was used. As entrepreneurs found wealth in mass production they also became greedy at the expense of workers, who were treated as a commodity instead of human beings. Attempts to correct poor working conditions via worker organizations often included violence.

The early founders of socialism did not define or provide any specific socialistic system. They largely noted the ills of the free enterprise system. A leading protester of capitalism, Robert Owen, has sometimes been called the father of socialism, but other than a few attempts at co-operative ventures, he added little to the establishment of any advanced socialistic system.

Karl Marx wrote "The Communist Manifesto" in

1848. He contended that the capitalistic system would create internal dissensions and would be destroyed from within. He believed that workers needed to revolt against industrialists and the governments that supported them. He essentially espoused revolutionary socialism or communism. Marx' writings were not widely read or given a great deal of credence until after his death, His views were later popularized by the Bolshevik revolution in Russia in the early twentieth century. Marx believed in a system of proletariat democracy but that was not the way it worked in Russia. Instead of the proletariat establishing the economic system the leaders of the communist party became the dictators who enforced their view of communism.

The Russia communist model indicated the problem with communism and future models contained the same flaws. Instead of power being vested in the workers or proletariat, the leaders of the country and of the communist party possessed the power and ruled with an iron fist and in a dictatorial manner. Communist governments in Soviet Union countries, China under Mao Zedong, Cuba, North Korea and a few others have seen power vested in a small number of leaders who take control of the government. The lot of workers in those countries has not been improved to any great extent and in most cases has become worse. The ownership of property tends to be owned or more rigidly controlled by the governments than is true in free enterprise countries. To this period in history, communism has not improved the lot of the worker beyond that achieved in countries that have a free enterprise system.

Marx' view of socialism or communism was somewhat different than was carried out in the communist countries. And to date a major problem with those countries is that freedom is suppressed and their economic systems have done little to improve the lot of workers.

One can argue that the countries with free enterprise systems have tended to be subjected to more and more government controls and regulations as such systems have grown. One can also argue that communism is an extreme example of socialism. One can also argue that many countries with free enterprise systems are today not the lassez-faire form of capitalism envisioned more than two hundred years ago. What these arguments say is that neither capitalism nor socialism tend to exist in pure form in the advanced economic nations of modern times.

Our country has drifted away from a totally free enterprise system. Government has placed more and more laws and regulations on businesses as we have progressed through history. Some of those laws and regulations are necessary. The never-ending question is to what extent government should intervene in the free enterprise system and what are the long-term consequences of such intervention.

But this conclusion can be made. If the principle our founding fathers set forth in the Declaration of Independence, that people are endowed with the inalienable right to freedom, than the free enterprise system best fits with that principle.

Chapter 3 --- Major Changes to Our Economic System

*A*t the time this country was founded "mercantilism" was the predominant economic system employed in the fledgling nation and also in most European countries. This system was based on the belief that the financial well being of a nation was dependent on its supply of capital. It also assumed that economic well-being was a zero sum game and that a nation needed a positive trade balance to stay on the positive side of the zero sum game. Positive trade balances led to protective trade tariffs and also to numerous European wars and imperialism.

One significance of mercantilism to our new country was that it helped lead to our Declaration of Independence because English mercantilism and its associated imperialistic practices were significant factors in the colonies' grievances against England.

At about the time we became a country, the economic system of mercantilism was fading as the arguments of

Adam Smith were beginning to prevail. The lassez-faire free market economy was taking roots in economically advanced nations.

Alexander Hamilton was the first Secretary of the Treasury of this nation and he was instrumental in initiating an economic policy for the country. Under his leadership at Treasury the fledgling nation assumed and retired the debt incurred by the states and the Continental Congress during the Revolutionary War. A national bank was created. Some tariffs were approved to raise revenues but some were also rejected.

The major economic venture of the young nation was farming and economic opportunities via government land grants and other means of obtaining land were numerous. Small towns with small entrepreneurs were also established. The common thread for all economic ventures was freedom to succeed or fail. It was a nation of opportunity for the entrepreneurs.

The immigrants who came to this country often came to escape oppressive governments and they cherished freedom. Freedom was an important societal and economic value. The private economic system was subjected to a minimal amount of government intervention in the way of laws and regulations. As the nation grew and the economic system became more complex, the degree of government intervention would change.

From its founding until the Civil War, this nation was primarily a rural and agrarian society. Federal government intervention in the form of laws and regulations was minimal.

The government's role in many areas was aiding the development of economic activity. Senator Henry Clay in the early nineteenth century proposed an "American System" that included the building of a national road, the imposition of tariffs to pay for the road and a second national bank. These proposals created political controversy and were generally defeated by the Congress or vetoed by the President. The national road was built between Cumberland, Maryland and Wheeling, West Virginia but was not of great significance as rivers began being used more for transportation along with canals which were built in a number of areas. In the mid-nineteenth century, railroads began being built and helped usher in the Industrial Revolution and interstate commerce.

The Civil War helped create the need for factories to supply war needs to both the North and the South. After the Civil War the transcontinental railroad was opened and it gave impetus to the industrialization of this nation. Along with industrialization came new business and economic opportunities and practices. Prior to industrialization most businesses were owned by a sole proprietor or by small partnerships. New ways of putting together larger business combinations, included corporations, trusts and holding companies. Larger factories were built by these larger business combinations and with these larger factories came economies of scale but also abuses in business practices, including monopolies. Advantage was taken of workers, in the form of excessively long hours, child labor and unsafe business practices.

It is an unfortunate flaw of man to be greedy and to treat other humans in manners one would not wish to be treated. Workers were too frequently treated as a commodity and with such treatment came worker abuses.

As is usually the case with abusive practices, they created the need for new laws and regulations. Some of the more significant laws included the establishment of the Interstate Commerce Commission in 1887. The Commission was given the power to regulate all aspects of interstate commerce. A few years later, Congress passed the Sherman Antitrust Act, which disallowed monopolies and restricted other companies from using unfair business practices. The intervention of the federal government began on a larger scale but with hindsight these restrictions on business practices were appropriate.

Was the free enterprise system affected? Yes, but not in a severely adverse manner. That was yet to come.

During the same period some tariffs were added to protect American businesses and to raise capital necessary for government functions. At various times, forms of income tax were also imposed but not on a large-scale basis. That too was yet to come.

As noted earlier the larger business combinations brought about labor abuses. In addition to difficult labor conditions, the workers also did not share in the wealth the business combinations generated. Early labor movements were only partially successful and often were more interested in moving to a more socialistic economic society than in correcting labor abuses and fighting for better wages. When Samuel Gompers became head of the American Federation of Labor (AFL) that changed. Gompers had no hidden agenda. His interests were to increase wages, reduce hours and improve working conditions. The AFL under his leadership obtained improvements for workers, which eventually led to the establishment of a large middle class in this country as wages were improved.

The positive effect of labor unions to our nation cannot be diminished. From unions came a middle class of people and from the middle class came consumers and from consumers came greater production. All of these added to our nation becoming more prosperous. The problem with unions occurs when greed replaces the right for competitive wages and wage demands become excessive. The problem of corporate management comes when greed replaces the right to a reasonable return and returns become excessive.

The early twentieth century began with more reforms. Under Presidents Theodore Roosevelt and William Howard Taft the powers of the Interstate Commerce Commission were broadened. The Commission was given the power to regulate railroads, pipelines, bridges, and terminals. Subsequently, the telephone and telegraph business also became subjected to the authority of the Commission.

As President Taft completed his one term in office, the sixteenth amendment to the United States Constitution was enacted. It is an amendment that would help make it possible to substantially alter our economic system, our individual lives and increase the power of government. The amendment ratified on February 3, 1913 stated, "The Congress shall have the power to lay and collect taxes on income, from whatever source derived, without apportionment among the several States and without regard to any census or enumeration." Later that year, tariffs would be lowered and a graduated income tax was created. The consequences of the federal income tax are so extensive that a later chapter will be dedicated exclusively to its impact.

Also in 1913, the Federal Reserve Board was established. In effect, it gave the government a national banking system. With the establishment of the Federal Reserve Board and its current 12 districts (each with a Federal Reserve Bank) the government obtained the ability to control the monetary supply of the country and issue new currency. Over the years the Federal Reserve Board has had a major impact on our economic system, as did the federal income tax. It too merits a chapter in this book.

The federal income tax, the Federal Reserve Board and our federal debt, are three of the greatest influences, the federal government has on our economic system. The Federal Reserve Board is included here, even though it is not directly controlled by the government. These three factors most assuredly can be said to have changed our more pure lassez-faire free enterprise system into a mixed economy of free enterprise with government oversight and regulation to ensure economic and social interests. Despite the increased government involvement we were not a socialistic economic system, because the free economic system continued without government ownership in it.

Another important piece of legislation was the Clayton

Antitrust Act of 1914. It permitted the government to regulate business practices that tried to prevent competition.

World War I caused an even greater intervention by government. It became necessary for the government to become involved in what and how much was produced as well as how to distribute food, and how to manage and transport supplies. It also became involved in the supervision of the telephone and telegraph services as well as other public utilities. The War Revenue Act, which was necessary to fund the war, provided for increased taxes and the sale of war bonds.

When the war ended there was a short economic downturn period as war production activities declined. But shortly after the small downturn the economy prospered. Boom periods are inclined to precipitate excesses and abuses and that was true in the 1920's. Excesses occurred in the area of stock purchases as investors were permitted to buy stock on the margin with the hopes that subsequent increases would allow payment of the debt incurred. The buying led to increases in the stock market, which were not sustainable, and in October 1929, the great crash of the market occurred. Margins could not be covered and caused many to file for bankruptcy. Banks were also affected and many failed.

Many factors contributed to the Great Depression but if one human factor was to blame it was probably the greed during the roaring 20's. Widespread greed tends to lead to excesses in the economy followed by business slumps. The economic impacts underscored the weak banking structure that was in place at the beginning of the Depression. The Federal Reserve Board did little to help the situation. International economies were generally weakened due to high tariffs and high levels of debt. There was no government regulation of stock market speculation. Farm prices around the world dropped substantially. Unemployment was widespread. Consumption of goods was reduced. The plight of people called for greater government intervention and greater government intervention was about to come.

President Herbert Hoover instituted a number of programs including the Reconstruction Finance Corporation which was intended to bail out railroads, mortgage companies and banks. He also used federal funds to start building projects in an attempt to put people back to work. His programs were not very effective.

In 1932 Franklin Roosevelt was elected president. He initiated a program, called the New Deal in order to get the economy back on track. His programs were intended to provide relief, recovery and reform. His numerous programs for relief included the Civilian Conservation

Corps, the Public Works Administration and the Works Progress Administration. All were designed to create employment for government projects.

His recovery programs also included the Federal Housing Administration which would provide insurance on home loans and the Tennessee Valley Authority, which was to provide cheaper electricity and flood protection throughout large areas of the South. Another recovery plan provided farm subsidies to farmers which were aimed at reducing production in order to support higher farm prices.

Roosevelt's New Deal also provided numerous reform legislation. The Federal Deposit Insurance Corporation was created to guarantee bank deposits. The Securities and Exchange Commission was created to help regulate stock exchanges and financial advisors. Reform legislation also included a safety net for seniors in the form of the Social Security Act, which was begun in 1935 and was to be funded through a payroll tax on employers and employees.

Some would call President's New Deal an entry into socialism, but that was not true in the strict meaning of the word because government did not take ownership in the free enterprise or capitalistic system of the country. Rather it could be called a mixed economy in which the free enterprise system would remain in place. But it would be a system that was more closely regulated by government for "social good". It would be fair to rename the economic system in 1940 a "socially regulated free enterprise system". And from a governmental standpoint we were certainly moving toward a social democracy. And yes, Mr. Franklin those who might be mischievous in the free enterprise system now had many masters in Washington. But too many masters can also be a problem.

After 1940, the question of concern should have been and should still be, "How much social regulation by government is appropriate in our capitalistic or free enterprise system"? If we want the inalienable right to freedom to remain a hallmark of our democracy, the answer should be that the least amount of government restrictions to the free enterprise system is best. That was debated then and it is debated now. The "invisible hand" theory of Adam Smith whereby the free system will be guided to produce the current and future wants and needs of consumers is still a good theory that can apply to our economic system of today.

Whether or not the New Deal program ended the Great Depression is still debated. The beginning of World War II no doubt contributed somewhat to the end of the Great Depression as probably did some of the New Deal Programs. How much each contributed was, is and will continue to be debated.

World War II increased the role of government in our economic system. Production for the defense industry provided more jobs for many people which for the first time included a large number of women. Government also had to ration numerous goods because it was necessary to utilize production facilities such as tires for the wartime effort. Rationing of food was also necessary. Government intervention, such as the War Production Board provided, was necessary to assure the readiness of our military effort.

With the end of World War II came prosperity in this nation. The United States also emerged as the strongest economy in the world. In addition to the economy being expanded, the United States also became instrumental in rebuilding the economies of foreign countries, whose production facilities had been ravaged by the war. The United States began to play the role of economic and military leader for the free world.

Following World War II, changes to society came at a more rapid pace. The population grew quickly after the war. The population growth required more schools and more consumer products. Suburbs began springing up outside of cities. The media via TV began bringing news to us more rapidly. The number of automobiles grew rapidly and the Interstate Highway System came into being. Air transportation via the jet made cross-country flying easily available. These changes were rapidly transforming the economic system, societal values and enlarging the role of government.

In 1963, Lyndon Johnson became president and initiated a program called the Great Society. It was an economic and social program that would further expand the role of government. His program included the spending of billions of dollars to improve and build schools. He created the Head Start program for early education. The Job Corps was created. The most significant new entitlement program was Medicare which provided health insurance to senior citizens who were 65 or older. Medicaid was also begun to help states provide health coverage otherwise not affordable.

Government also became involved in worker safety in factories, in fighting pollution and in other programs to benefit the country. While the free enterprise system was still a capitalistic system the role of government in the economic system was substantial and the size of government was growing rapidly. Yes Mr. Franklin, we now had even more masters. Masters here, masters there, masters everywhere.

In the late 1960's and throughout the 1970's the country suffered from high inflation rates. During the Carter administration the country went through a period called stagflation which included high inflation rates, high unemployment rates and a stagnant economy.

In 1980, the country elected the conservative president, Ronald Reagan. In the area of economics, the Reagan administration operated on the belief of supply side economics, with the view that if taxes were cut for businesses and high income individuals they would invest the savings in the economy thus providing stimulation to the economy. Reagan also wanted to reduce the size of government and balance the budget, but increased spending made the latter impossible. The level of the federal debt was increased during Reagan's two terms. During his administration the Cold War would be wound down.

For the balance of the twentieth century, the country generally prospered with the exception of a mild slowdown in the early 1990s. Technological innovation was responsible for much of the prosperity and it was also helping to streamline industry and improve productivity. Another change to the economy was the outsourcing of much of the manufacturing base of this nation. The impact of that is yet to be determined although recent years seem to indicate such outsourcing has had a negative impact on our economy. As we entered the twenty-first century the manufacturing factories of America no longer required the high percentage of workers who were necessary through most of the twentieth century. High technology businesses and the service industry have replaced manufacturing as the part of the economy that provides most jobs for Americans.

At the beginning of this book we identified the two events that have most recently influenced the economy in the United States; the terrorist attacks on September 11, 2001 that caused our military involvement in two countries together with the war on terrorism and the most severe recession since the Great Depression. This latest recession can again find its roots in greed and incompetent financial transactions. Although they were different in nature, greed was the similar ingredient that gave rise to the Great Depression and the more current Great Recession. Irresponsible mortgage lending, uncontrolled and irresponsible financial instruments and irresponsible levels of debt in all areas of the economy led to the deep recession which is still somewhat ongoing as this book is being written.

Government programs, including health care, continue to grow - government regulations continue to expand - government spending continues to accelerate - government deficits are monumental - and government debt is larger than ever. Ah yes, Mr. Franklin, we still need masters. Maybe we don't need them but occasionally greedy people deserve them, and the rest of society suffers the consequences.

In the 230 plus years of this country, we have truly evolved from a very pure free enterprise or capitalistic system to a very mixed economy of the free enterprise system and an ever-growing involvement of the federal government in the economic system. It is now a heavily socially regulated capitalistic system. In 1998 a Joint Economic Committee of Congress issued a study on "Government Size and Economic Growth". The study indicated that economic growth may be hampered when there is no government involvement but it could also be hampered with too much government involvement. What is the right amount of government involvement and which involvement matters? The history of governments has never provided the perfect answer. All governments have failed.

The following governmental interventions have all played a significant role in the economy of this nation and may play a greater role in the future:

- The amount of laws and regulations controlling economic activity

- Taxation on businesses and individuals and the progressivity of such taxes

- The gargantuan amount of federal debt

- The staggering amount of unfunded liabilities relating to entitlement programs

- The Federal Reserve Board and Federal Reserve System

It is not only government intervention that affects an economy but also workers, productivity, management of businesses, greed, financial astuteness and other factors. However this book is primarily a study of the manner in which the government has affected the economy and we are limiting most of our analysis to the major factors of government intervention. There are so many factors that it is doubtful that anyone can pinpoint to any specific area of government intervention that most affected the economy. In the next few chapters we will look at some of the most significant factors. The immediate next chapter will focus on the monumental increase in government itself.

Chapter 4 --- The Growth of the Federal Government

In his autobiography, Thomas Jefferson noted, "It is not by the consolidation or concentration, of powers, BUT BY THEIR DISTRIBUTION, that good government is effected". During the recent history of our federal government, it does not appear that there are many disciples of Jefferson's view residing in Washington, D.C. We have a federal government that has steadily consolidated power in Washington. In this chapter we will review how that has come about and in later chapters how the people, the culture and the economy of this nation have been "effected" and transformed.

In chapter one, we reviewed the importance our founding fathers placed on faith-based morality. Our founders were not only cognizant of what provided the best government, but also understood the moral philosophy that was necessary to make such a government possible. Big government consolidates power and that alone undermines the founding fathers moral philosophy, because power tends to corrupt and also infringes on the inalienable right to freedom for individuals. As power increases in Washington, the freedom for citizens tends to erode.

Jefferson summarized well the role of government in his inaugural address, "A wise and frugal government, which shall restrain men injuring one another, SHALL LEAVE THEM OTHERWISE FREE TO REGULATE THEIR OWN PURSUITS OF INDUSTRY AND IMPROVEMENT, and shall not take from the mouth of labor the bread it has earned; this is the sum of good government, and this is necessary to close the circle of our felicities." Some of our felicities have been relegated to the ashes of history.

Jefferson was a great political philosopher. One additional statement of his, which was noted earlier, summarizes the transformation and growth of the federal government. "The natural progress of things is for liberty to yield and government to gain ground". That is a good summary of the history of our nation.

The role for the government of this nation was wonderfully conceived by our founding fathers, including the moral philosophy that would ensure its continuity. But far too often in the past 236 years our federal government has forgotten the words of our first president. "Virtue or morality must be the springboard to popular government." He also indicated that it is faith-based morality that provides good government.

In the early years of our federal government, citizens were generally provided extensive freedom to self regulate "their own pursuits of industry and improvement". In the prior chapter we noted the interventions of government in our economy over the course of our history. We also noted the Joint Commission Study that indicated too little government could hamper economic growth, as could too much government. Let us now look at the effects of the growing intervention by the federal government which extends into all aspects of the lives of the people, the economy and the social fabric of this nation. Because government, if anything, is too large, our concern will focus on the excessive involvement of government. Too little government does not hamper us.

Until the Industrial Revolution, which primarily began after the Civil War, our government with minor exceptions left men and enterprise free to regulate their own pursuits. Thereafter, some of the abuses of industrialization called for government intervention. The reforms enacted in the late nineteenth and early twentieth century were appropriate to ensure "the bread for labor that it had earned". These reforms also helped ensure that business structures would not have an unfair advantage via trusts and monopolies. These trusts and monopolies were simply too powerful and the regulations imposed by government were necessary to ensure such power would not be abusive and which in fact had become abusive.

It is difficult for the government to become excessive without a tax system, duties or tariffs to pay for the excesses. One of the early errors in our system may be attributed to the passage of the Sixteenth Amendment permitting the imposition of income taxes without any limitations on the amount or utilization of such taxes. In a free enterprise system the capital for growth is generated by that free enterprise system. When taxes on corporations and individuals become excessive, the capital needed for growth is transferred to government. If government then does not invest such capital with the same growth capabilities, as would the free enterprise system, the rate of growth diminishes. That is simple economics. Income taxes and unbridled federal debt have become two factors which have and will continue to hamper the economic growth of this nation. As noted earlier, the issue of taxes is so significant that it will be dealt with in a separate chapter.

The Sixteenth Amendment, as aforementioned, was ratified in 1913 and in that same year the Federal Reserve Board was established. The latter's creation was needed to manage the financial aspects of our economic system. Its actions during the Great Depression may not have been what it should have been, but it has served the financial and economic systems very well during most of its existence. In many ways it is more effective than many of the government programs that are often initiated during recessionary periods. Its role too is so significant to this nation's economic system that it also will be dealt with in a separate chapter.

The system we refer to as Social Security began with the Social Security Act of 1935. It came into being for good reasons but some aspects of it are not good. That system today is in financial jeopardy and needs to be reformed. Before tackling that issue a legitimate question could be raised as to the degree of social entitlement involvement that is necessary by the federal government. Was the Social Security Act "a wise and frugal government" involvement? The question of Social Security can be split into two issues - the first being the need of the system and the second being the financing and administration of the system.

At the time the Social Security Act was passed there was a need for such a safety net. As we became a more urban and mobile society, senior citizens who were no longer being cared for by family members needed income for their retirement years. It did not appear to be a great financial risk for government because the average mortality age at that time was sixty-five. But as people lived longer the financial drain on the system became greater.

The error made by government was its decision to be the sole administrator of the system. Senior citizens and the government would have been better served if a private system or private corporation administered the system, in much the same manner as defined pension benefit plans would be administered in the future. Considering the amount of taxes contributed by the employee and the employer, the return to the retiree should be better. In addition, the unfunded liability, which now exists at the federal government level, could have been avoided, because the additional earnings that a private system could have earned would have been enough to avoid the unfunded liability that has been incurred by the federal government. The government could guarantee these payments by the private system through The Employee Retirement Income Security Act in the same way they do the private pension system.

It is not by the consolidation or concentration, of powers, BUT BY THEIR DISTRIBUTION, that good government is effected. The federal government does not have a good track record as regards the administration of much of anything. There is a reason for that. Too often in government, proper authority, responsibility and accountability are lacking. Such traits are important in the private sector. The acceptance of responsibility and accountability are not traits of politicians who serve as our elected officials. They are better at blaming others.

There have been many critics of the federal programs initiated during the Great Depression. I am not among those critics. Drastic conditions do take drastic steps. I do not know if the private economy on its own could have eliminated the Depression without government intervention or how much longer it would have taken, and we will never know the answer to that question. World War II may also have been an important factor in ending the Depression.

When a nation faces a Depression, government's role tends to expand, and if that expansion is temporary it is a proper role of government, because it can help ensure that the worker who becomes unemployed has "bread on the table". However, government's role in such emergencies should be temporary, but that is rarely the case.

During World War II this nation incurred substantial deficits in order to fund the war. I also find no fault in those temporary deficits. The continuing freedom of our own citizens and that of many other people in other countries was at stake and the monumental effort to protect that freedom justified the huge deficits. The danger again is that certain programs initiated during wars are not always eliminated just as measures to eliminate recessions are not always eliminated.

During the 1960's, under the Administration of President Lyndon Johnson, many government programs were initiated under the broad banner of The Great Society. The goals were numerous and included programs to eliminate poverty and racial injustice. Spending programs also were initiated to address education, medical care and other societal issues.

The Great Society programs were generally an overreach by the federal government, but the civil rights acts of 1964 and 1965 were long needed and have done much to correct racial injustices in this nation. The funding of education by the federal government has done little, if anything, to help educational problems. It has also contributed to making the cost of education very expensive.

Legislation establishing Medicare is proving to be a financial burden on the government that is unsustainable. The unfunded liability of that program now stands in the tens of trillions of dollars. Eventually the financial problems of Social Security and Medicare will need to be addressed. Those programs were ill planned and subsequent financing problems have proven that point. Opening the federal checkbook without limitations is an invitation to financial disaster in addition to being a false promise. In both education and Medicare the federal government again ignored Thomas Jefferson's words on assuming powers or programs that should not be in the domain of government.

During the remainder of the twentieth century the federal government continued to grow. Growth has included many more regulations and laws. Some administrations have been guiltier than others but in general all contributed to some degree to the increase in federal programs and regulations as well as in the national debt.

In the twenty-first century thus far, the national debt has increased at an alarming rate. It increased significantly under the Bush Administration and has increased even more during the Obama Administration.

As some of the regulations came in the form of added costs to business, manufacturers in the United States began looking for ways to cut costs. That included outsourcing of jobs to foreign countries and the percentage of manufacturing jobs began dwindling. The bright spot to manufacturing came in the form of new breakthroughs in technology in the 1990's. They were accompanied by economic prosperity and a few rare years of surpluses in the federal budget.

In the first twelve years of the twenty-first century,

the two events noted in the Introduction of this book occurred. The impacts of the terrorists destruction on 9/11/01 and the Great Recession that began in 2008 are still being felt and will continue to have an impact for years to come. It is likely that the federal debt may quadruple in the fifteen-year period of 2002 to 2017. We will try to put the effects of that into some perspective in later chapters of this book.

With the Affordable Health Care Act and other programs which the Obama administration enacted early in its administration the national debt of the country may approximate or exceed $20 trillion by 2017. That debt alone would equate to more than $60,000 for every person living in this country at the present time. When the unfunded liabilities of Social Security and Medicare are added to the national debt along with the debt of federal agencies and state governments, the amount of debt is staggering when viewed on a per capita basis. Future ramifications will include a severe financial burden for the federal government, which will in turn mean financial burdens for future generations in the form of high levels of taxation or inflation or both.

The rapid growth in government has transformed our nation. It is also making us a poorer nation.

All the warnings about big government that Thomas Jefferson enumerated have been thrown to the wind.

Government is big and it is powerful. It has not distributed power as Jefferson suggested it should, but rather it has consolidated power. Government, through legislation and regulation, is now intrusive in the lives of its citizens and in the free enterprise system. Taxation is burdensome for all. We cannot exactly forecast the effects of such an increased role by the federal government, but in the next chapters we will try to better evaluate and project some likely outcomes of the increased role of government.

Chapter 5 --- The Impact of Federal Income Taxes

In an earlier book, I used an alleged quotation that has been attributed to a Professor Alexander Tyler which was made in regards to the Athenian Republic. It follows:

"A democracy cannot exist as a permanent form of government. It can only exist until the voters discover that they can vote themselves money from the public treasury. From that moment on, the majority always votes for the candidates promising the most money from the public treasury, with the result that a democracy always collapses over loose fiscal policy followed by a dictator. The average age of the world's great civilizations has been two hundred years. These nations have progressed through the following sequence: from bondage to spiritual faith, from spiritual faith to great courage, from courage to liberty, from liberty to abundance, from abundance to selfishness, from selfishness to complacency, from complacency to apathy, from apathy to dependency, from dependency back to bondage."

These words were supposedly written in the middle of the eighteenth century. It is interesting that they would have been written before capitalism or socialism were defined as economic systems. They would also have been written during periods when kings and queens were more frequently involved in the governance of people. However, even when one substitutes the more modern forms of government, some truth remains to the above alleged quotation. People may not be returned to bondage as the alleged Professor Tyler may have thought of bondage, but they may be returned to a different form of subservience.

In this nation there is certainly some truth to the fact that people vote for those who promise to deliver most from the public treasury, and all too frequently do it without understanding that their taxes will be the source of the income needed by the public treasury to pay for the promises made to them. Therefore to those who demand more, i.e. the public, more will be demanded from them in the form of taxes. If that was the only problem it would not be too bad, provided that those who paid the taxes received their fair allocation back from government. But that is not the way it works. Once the government receives taxes they use or reapportion them, as they deem appropriate. It is that power thing that Jefferson warned about. It is a redistribution of the wealth of a nation. It is also the siphoning off of capital that might otherwise be used for economic growth.

Not all is bad about taxes. We need federal money for roads, bridges and other infrastructure needs. We need defensive protection. We need a few other things that can best be done by government.

But when we demand more, government tries to provide more, because that unfortunately is how the politicians in a democracy get elected. That greater demand is also why government needs to progressively increase taxes. The greater inflow of tax revenue is how power becomes consolidated at the federal level and that is a real danger. The vicious circle of higher demands and higher taxation is how people return to bondage or rather how in modern times they become subservient to the rulers in Washington. That is also how this wonderfully conceived government that initially wished to decentralize and distribute power has been altered.

Let us take a look at the relatively brief history of federal taxation in this nation. It should not be surprising that as taxes increased so did the Federal government. Taxation is permitted in the Constitution. Section 8 of the Constitution states the following: "The Congress shall have the Power to lay and collect Taxes, Duties, Imposts and Excises, to pay the Debts and provide for the common Defence and general Welfare of the United States; but all Duties, Imposts, and Excises shall be uniform throughout the United States:".

Until the Civil War income taxes were not necessary for the Federal government. Its role remained fairly small and what income was necessary was able to be satisfied through the impositions of duties, tariffs and some other minor taxes. In order to fund the Civil War, it was necessary for the Congress to pass the Revenue Act of 1861. It was a benign flat income tax of three percent on income above $800. A year later the Revenue Act of 1862 replaced the 1861 Act. It levied a graduated tax of three to five percent on income above $600. It did another important thing. It placed a termination date of 1866 on the tax.

In the latter part of the nineteenth century various political parties at times advocated income taxes. Late in that century, a case that went to the Supreme Court, Pollack v. Farmers' Loan and Trust Co. declared certain taxes to be unconstitutionally apportioned. Without getting into the complexity of the case suffice it to say that the Sixteenth Amendment negated the Supreme Court's declaration. The Sixteenth Amendment as noted earlier was ratified in 1913. It permitted taxes on income without apportionment among the several States, and without regard to any census or enumeration, which also was an issue in the Pollack case. The Sixteenth Amendment gave Congress the unbridled ability to levy and increase taxes as it saw fit and it now has the capability to utilize the proceeds as it sees fit.

Until the early part of the twentieth century, the need for any income taxation had been minor. That would change as the century progressed. Taxes were levied to pay for World War I and were substantially increased during the Great Depression. They would subsequently be needed to pay for more and more federally administered programs. And so the role of government increased. Why not? It now discovered it had the necessary power to tax, spend and expand. It is not only government's fault that taxes and government increase. People keep asking for the government to do more. Remember the words of Professor Tyler.

Toward the end of World War I income taxes became more and more progressive and by the end of the war the tax rate for the highest income level reached seventy-one percent of income. With the boom of the 1920's, taxes were lowered a number of times and the top rate was eventually reduced to twenty-five percent.

As government initiated many programs during the Depression of the 1930's, government made the mistake of also raising taxes in an attempt to pay for the numerous programs that were initiated. That action did not help the economy recover.

During World War II income taxes were necessary to pay for the war. But after the war ended income taxes did not go away. Without going through the rest of tax history through the present time suffice it to say income taxes at high levels have become a part of life in the United States. And with the increase in taxes came the inevitable increase in government, and with the increase in government came the increase in power of politicians in Washington. Our elected officials in Washington did and still do what Jefferson warned them not to do. They consolidated and concentrated power in Washington. The distribution of power is no longer much of a consideration by those who are in power.

It is the income tax system, more than anything else, which finances the move to bigger government and the consolidation of power in Washington. As government moves toward a more socially regulated economy, it also begins limiting the potential for growth in a free enterprise system. It is an economic fact, that as income is taken from citizens and businesses to finance government programs, it diminishes the capital available for economic growth. One can of course also argue that some social security safety nets are necessary for the common good of all citizens. Those are the two sides of the taxation coin. On one side taxation limits economic growth and on the other side it provides social programs in numerous forms to a broader base of all the people. The risk in trying to provide a broader safety net for everyone is that everyone may become poorer in the process.

These then are the questions that all Americans should ask of themselves and their representatives. At what point does taxation stifle growth to the extent that it reduces the standard of living for the poor as well as the wealthy? At what point does taxation stifle incentive for the entrepreneur to create wealth? Adam Smith might also ask at what point does the invisible hand of free enterprise disappear and become replaced by the mighty arm of government? And finally how much does taxation erode freedom?

We have examples of the former Soviet Union countries, Cuba, North Korea, China during the days of Mao, and other nations where governments are totally socialistic and economic enterprises are government owned. They were not only economic failures but they also restricted the freedom of their citizens. The United States prior to World War I was at the other extreme, inasmuch as government played a very small role in the economic system. Our country thrived under that system. It also minimized the consolidation of power in Washington. There is no proof that increases in taxes and in government power are an overall benefit to the citizens of a country. There is some evidence to the contrary.

Jefferson had it exactly right when he noted that effective government was a government that distributed power. Government can legislate a social security system that can be administered by and financed through the free enterprise system. Government can legislate a health system that can be administered by the free enterprise system. Government can initiate other programs that can also be delegated or distributed to free enterprise or state governments. The Social Security System and the Medicare System have been poorly administered and are in terrible financial condition.

It is not the role of government to be the nanny overseer of all citizens. Its role is to ensure the safety and freedom of its citizens and ensure an environment where all citizens are treated equally, and that the "care of all humans' life and happiness" is not denied by government.

The ineffective administration by government of what can be good programs has also centralized power in Washington and is bankrupting our nation. Entitlement programs and the interest on the federal debt require a substantial percentage of the total revenues of the federal government and that percentage continues to grow. As they continue to grow, federal government will have no choice but to maintain a high level of taxes on all citizens. Future generations will be forced to pay thousands of dollars per capita just to finance the interest on the national debt without receiving any benefits whatsoever. Even if no other federal programs exist, government will still need to tax citizens just to be able to pay interest on the national debt. Satisfying the wants of one generation and letting future generations pay for those wants is properly referred to as greed and greed tears away the fabric of our value system.

We have reached the point of increased subservience for citizens because they are forced to not only pay taxes but to pay them for interest on debt incurred without receiving any benefits in return. And in our modern form of government it is Professor Tyler's description of bondage. It also consolidates power in Washington. Those who implore and elect politicians to use more of the public treasury for greater increases in programs are also asking for a greater degree of bondage for their children and grandchildren. We are already subservient to some degree and it is likely that subservience will increase for future generations. The impact on those future generations seems to be forgotten or ignored.

The government has not only managed to spend all tax revenues but they have also managed to indebt the nation to a degree that it will have no choice but to tax people in order to service the debt of the nation. That will be necessary even if no other programs are initiated. It will not matter much which political party is in power. The programs that cannot be financed by the taxes of the current generation are programs that must be financed by more and more federal debt and will become the financial burden of future generations.

Ultimately this country may not be able to increase its debt without some limitations due to the reduced faith and creditworthiness of our debt. But the debt that has been and will be incurred will cause future taxpayers to pay them and thereby almost certainly ensure a nation that will be poorer in the future.

Countries in Europe are already experiencing severe restrictions on increasing their debt. Greece has been one example and others may follow.

Not only will the interest on the debt of the country become a severe problem in the future, but so will the Social Security and Medicare systems which have staggering unfunded liabilities. They too will have to be changed with people needing to work longer before retirement, receiving lesser benefits, paying higher taxes or some combination thereof.

Medicare is so underfunded that health care will have to be cut, rationed or reduced in some manner. Government will undoubtedly also try to raise taxes but eventually that solution alone will not be enough. If the national debt continues to grow as it has grown in the past few years, interest costs on the national debt could become so large that even Social Security and Medicare could eventually be substantially curtailed.

In 2009, the government enacted legislation that

provides for a new and broader health care system. It is an admirable goal to provide all citizens with health care. But it is also a goal that may jeopardize the best health care system in the world. It may also add additional debt and additional financial burden for future generations. It will certainly require additional taxation. There are no free lunches and there is no free health care.

The increasing level of taxes necessary to pay the interest on our national debt will not be taxation without representation for future generations but it will be taxation without benefits for anyone except those who hold the debt instruments, including foreign nations to whom we will pay the interest on the US indebtedness they hold. At this time in our history one of those nations is China. At some point our citizens may not only be subservient to the powers of Washington, but the powers of Washington may become subservient to foreign powers.

The onset of taxation is an indicator that a country is ready to move away from a pure free enterprise system and a pure democracy to a more socially regulated economic system and a socially regulated form of democracy. As taxes increase the degree of social regulation also tends to increase.

Last, but not least, taxation is corrupting our political representatives in Washington. They not only have the power to allocate the trillions of dollars received annually by the federal government but they have the power to allocate those dollars for immoral and useless purposes. They gradually become dictatorial in the process. Sometimes freedom is lost suddenly when a government is overthrown but sometimes freedom is lost gradually as more and more power is placed in the hands of our elected officials.

Chapter 6 --- The Staggering Federal Debt

Many of the problems associated with income taxes are also present with national debt. In addition, when federal debt becomes excessive it not only adversely impacts the citizens of a nation, but also negatively affects the nation's standing within the world community. As our country has increased its national debt at alarming rates in the past few years, the value of the dollar has declined relative to other currencies.

As this chapter is being updated, the national federal debt exceeds $16,000,000,000,000. That is $16 trillion. It is approximately $50,000 per every US citizen. It is truly staggering. It is mind-boggling. The $50,000 per citizen is about the same as the average personal debt of each citizen.

Irresponsible is an understatement. But who is responsible? Each of us must look in the mirror to answer a part of that question. In a democracy we vote for those who are directly responsible so we voters are indirectly responsible. We want more and more from government, which is irresponsible, so our representatives in Washington try to provide what it is we want, which too is irresponsible, especially when they don't understand or ignore the consequences of their action. It is their job to understand the consequences and legislate accordingly.

Remember Professor Tyler. We are doing our best to fulfill his predictions regarding a democracy. One might think that the biggest concern of government today would be how to begin the attempt to reduce the debt through reduced spending or an increase in taxes. Those, plus growth in the economy which can increase revenues, are the only direct ways for debt to be reduced. There is another indirect way of reducing debt. Higher future rates of inflation can in effect reduce debt when valued in today's dollar. By devaluing the dollar, high inflation in effect does lower the debt. But, inflation is another form of taxation on citizens. As government debt is increased at accelerated rates, the danger of higher inflation in the future becomes more likely.

Let us examine some measures that could be taken to reduce the national debt. As noted above one way is through an increase in taxes. If each Americans' (including all men, women and children) taxes were increased $500 per year, it would take more than 100 years to eliminate the debt. Let us assume you are a family of four. That means that by paying your share of the debt, you have to lower your spending by $2000 per year so you can help eliminate the debt over the next 100 years and that assumes no interest. We would still need to pay the taxes we pay today for the other federal government programs that currently exist.

If on the other hand we want to eliminate the $16 trillion in debt by reducing government expenditures, spending needs to be reduced by $160,000,000,000 per year for the next 100 years. Time for government to get started. Right?

Wrong!!! Instead of worrying about cutting spending, government's current plans are to continue spending at high levels over the next five years and by then have a national debt that will be in the vicinity of $20 trillion. And that forecast includes raising some taxes. That is following Professor Tyler's path of progression toward the termination of a democracy.

Could we begin to reduce the national debt? Yes, but the pain would have to be shared by all Americans to some degree. It would mean that all of us would need to quit looking to Washington for solutions. It would mean working to an older age which can be done - it would mean reducing the cost of education substantially which can be done - it would mean fewer trips to the doctor and other reduced spending for health care which can be done - it would mean being more responsible for our health which can be done - it would mean saving more which can be done - it would mean voting for those who favor fiscally responsible solutions to "problems" which can be done. But will these steps be taken? Probably not until a financial crisis becomes imminent or a reality.

It is the flawed nature of humans to always want more and government always tries to deliver more than it responsibly can. At some point as noted earlier the federal government may be unable to sell debt or at least do so without high levels of interest and that could require drastic curtailments in spending, which in turn might trigger some of the aforementioned curtailments that would then be necessary in order to reduce or at least stabilize the amount of federal debt.

We are beginning to see financial crises in other debt-laden countries. It could happen here and how that might impact us will be addressed later in this book. The trigger that could create a crisis may be the inability of the federal government to continue selling debt instruments as has been done in the past or the refusal of other nations to use the US dollar as an international currency.

In recent years conservatives have followed a belief that by cutting taxes we can get the economy to grow more rapidly and thereby generate more revenue because of increased income and thus reduce the deficit. All of that is true to some degree but that has not happened. In the past thirty years the more conservative presidents and congresses have cut taxes on several occasions but federal spending and the federal deficits were also increased during those periods. It is difficult in a democracy to reduce spending.

Liberals on the other hand tend to favor more spending on social programs and favor raising taxes on corporations (corporations don't vote) and the higher income people of America to pay for such spending. But during the terms of liberal presidents and congresses we too have run deficits.

The opiate of the people seems to be the demand for services from government and the opiate of government seems to be to deliver those services and let fiscal responsibility be ignored. Yes, Professor Tyler, we seem to like that path you described. Let us not talk too much about fiscal responsibility but rather let us have some things we cannot afford. Let us be honest about it. Taxes and federal deficits pay for things we want even if our nation cannot afford them and some of the things we want we do not need.

Is there a middle ground that would slow down this seemingly endless and irresponsible increase in the national debt? Yes, including some noted earlier in this chapter, but it may be more financial medicine than we are willing to take.

To begin resolving our financial problems may necessitate the acknowledgment that there are limitations on the world leadership role we play and on the limitations the government can play in providing social programs for citizens. Limitations on wants and limitations on the role of government go against flawed human instincts and the flawed concept of great national power by politicians.

The responsible solution would be having some reductions in the level of debt, reducing and changing the administration of some social programs, recognize we cannot be the world's cop to every situation, recognize we cannot continue to provide the "nanny state" at the present level, and probably have some level of reduced economic growth as a result of the reductions in debt. None are financial medicines we like. There is almost no discussion of such financial medicine in government circles. Even the news media does not like to dwell on our limitations. It is not only through ignorance that our economic problems are ignored. It is cowardice. It is unfortunately a by-product of a democracy.

There is a great deal of hypocritical discussion by government and by the media about corporations and individuals needing to be more fiscally responsible. As this is being written we are slowly emerging from a terrible recession caused by the irresponsible amount of credit taken on by individuals and by corporations, especially financial corporations. Much of the criticism is warranted, but it never seems to be self-directed. It is more newsworthy to direct outrage at the compensation of corporate executives, than it is to examine the financial and other perks of politicians, the salaries of news commentators, the salaries of leading sports figures or the salaries of entertainment figures. Double standards are the standard of the day.

Via bailouts and stimulus packages, the irresponsible results caused by the actions of some individuals and some major corporations were assumed by the federal government on the irresponsible assumption that the government is too big to fail. It is flawed thinking to assume that any corporation may be too big to be permitted to fail. It is also flawed thinking to assume that the federal government cannot fail fiscally.

Credit rating agencies have already reduced their ratings on the instruments of the US governments' debt and if the debt continues to increase further reductions are likely.

As indicated earlier, the US dollar is also the currency used for the settlement of international transactions. If the US government permits debt to get to irresponsible levels, it could cause other nations to rebel against such use of the US dollar. That in turn could trigger worldwide economic panic.

It is true that nations or at least the soil on which they exist do not disappear, but governments while not disappearing from the lands they govern may surely fail or substantially change. That has been true from the beginning of time to the present time.

We have noted a few actions that should be taken and could spend considerable more time discussing the responsible actions that need to be taken by individuals, corporations and government. Unfortunately, that is not the road likely to be taken by flawed human beings. Greed is too major a flaw.

Professor Tyler was correct. It is the history of democracies to fail. But that is not the entire story. It is also the history of autocracies and other forms of government to fail. In the debate now taking place in this nation, the debate is whether or not more or less capitalism is needed or whether or not more or less socialism is needed. In my view, that is only a small part of the proper debate.

It is not just the form of government that fails, but it is the shortcoming of humans and the shortcomings of governments combined, which cause governments to fail. In this country, it is my view, that the major reason for failure is departing from the moral vision our founding fathers had of what makes for a great people and a great government. There are many who do not share that view and they are probably a majority in this country.

In these two chapters on taxes and federal debt, the failures attributable to both have been noted. As we listen to politicians today we hear many of the same debates we heard in the 1960's. At that time we initiated the "Great Society" programs that were going to resolve many, if not all of the ills of that time - education, health care, and others. Today, we are again trying to resolve those same type problems through spending money we don't have.

As noted in the prior chapter, taxation moves a country toward a more socially regulated free enterprise system. The same can also be said when government incurs higher levels of debt. But debt is even worse. It is a guarantee that future economic growth will be restricted, as government requires more of the capital to service the debt which would otherwise be available for economic growth. The incurrence of high levels of interest ensures a poorer nation in the future.

In these two chapters on taxes and on the debt we have

briefly examined their failures. The inalienable right to freedom granted to human beings is diminished by taxes and federal debt. It makes citizens subservient to government and that is backwards. It is government that should be subservient to citizens.

Freedom is a right bestowed on us by our Creator that should extend to every person on earth. It is an inalienable right. That inalienable right of freedom also extends to the entrepreneurs of our country. Taxes and federal debt erode that precious right. Through taxes and federal debt government gains grounds and liberty yields. Jefferson was right.

Chapter 7 --- The Growing Role of the Federal Reserve

In Chapter 4 we noted the areas of government growth and periods during which government grew rapidly. In Chapters 5 and 6 we noted that taxes and debt have had much to do with the growth of our federal government and the consolidation of power in Washington. Despite government growth, higher taxes and higher government debt, the citizens of this country still maintain a high level of freedom, albeit less than that enjoyed by prior generations. A real danger of bigger government is the tendency to increase intervention in the lives of Americans and the free enterprise system and in the process gradually diminish freedom.

Before we examine the role of the Federal Reserve over the course of its history, let us summarize the four areas we believe have led most to the harmful growth and transformation of our federal government:

1. Excessive levels of income taxes which fund the growth of government, help consolidate and

concentrate the power of the federal government, and utilize capital that otherwise would be available for economic growth. According to US Debt Clock. org. in December, 2012, the annual revenues of the federal government approximated $2.5 trillion or almost $8,000 per US citizen. That does not include the approximate $2.6 trillion of revenues for state and local government which would also be about another $8,000 per US citizen.

2. Excessive increases in the national debt which also fund the growth of federal government and consolidate the power of federal government. In addition it harms the creditworthiness of our government and makes us dependent on foreign nations to help fund our debt. Finally the large amount of interest on the debt will require taxes on current and future generations of Americans, to pay the interest for which no benefits are received. In December, 2012, the federal debt was approximately $16.4 trillion or $52,000 per US citizen.

3. The Social Security System, which in concept is fine, could be administered more capably by the private enterprise system. Because it is underfunded it too will require more taxes, more debt and/or a reduction in benefits. In December, 2012 the unfunded liability of Social Security was approximately $16 trillion or a little over $50,000 per US citizen.

4. Medicare, which in concept too is fine, also needs better administration and is in need of reform if it is to remain viable. The current promises of the Social Security System and the Medicare System exceed the government's capability of financing those systems in the future, as presently structured. In December, 2012 the unfunded liability of Medicare, including the Part D Drug liability, was estimated to exceed $105 trillion or about $333,000 per every US citizen.

It is difficult for many citizens of this country to relate to the massive amount of indebtedness and unfunded liabilities which our government has incurred. We hear about the dangers of government indebtedness but to date the average citizen's life has not been severely affected.

So how can we explain the financial dangers to which our government has subjected us and future citizens? I tried to explain it by putting the indebtedness in terms of the amount incurred by our government per each US citizen. Eventually the citizens of this country are responsible for the debt and unfunded liabilities incurred by the government. It is true that corporations pay taxes but it is also true their taxes are passed on to the consuming public, i.e. the taxpayer.

Let us take another look at the indebtedness our Federal government has incurred on behalf of each one of the

315 million US citizens (as of Dec. 2012). If we add together each citizens' share of the federal debt ($52,000) plus the unfunded liability of Social Security ($50,000 per citizen) and the unfunded liability of Medicare ($333,000) the total comes to $435,000.

It is hard to comprehend the meaning of the above paragraph. Let us assume that each citizen attempted to obtain a loan for their $435,000. Even if a bank could be found that would be imprudent enough to make such a loan, it would cause more than 90% of the citizens of this country to be eligible for bankruptcy.

If you think your representatives in the federal government have represented you responsibly, please read again from the beginning of this chapter to this sentence.

The first sentence of this book's Introduction obtains a quote from our third president, Thomas Jefferson, which states, "the care of human life and happiness and not their destruction is the first and only legitimate object of good government". Unfortunately, in recent years the financial "destruction" of human life and happiness seems to be a role of government.

There are, of course, other problems with an excessively powerful federal government, but the aforementioned four economic issues are most troublesome at the present time and will be the most burdensome to future generations.

Unfortunately, the massive indebtedness incurred by the federal government has forced the Federal Reserve into a new role which will be reviewed later in this chapter.

The Federal Reserve System is a quasi-government system that, until recently, has worked for the benefit of the American people. It will soon be 100 years old and has generally served this country very well. In many ways it has served to provide the stimulant, which Keynes believed was occasionally necessary for a free enterprise system. It has also been reasonably effective for the most part in slowing down economic growth when growth became excessive. And for most of its existence it has been helpful in preventing excessive inflation or deflation. Its future role will be critical to this nation.

As previously noted, Congress established the Federal Reserve in 1913 when it enacted the Federal Reserve Act. The initial motivation to establish the Federal Reserve was to prevent banking-caused financial panics. Prior to 1913 there had been several banking panics. An especially severe panic occurred in 1907 which was the crisis that led to the passage of the Act in 1913.

The Federal Reserve System is responsible for numerous functions including the following:

- Serving as the United States' central bank

- Maintaining financial stability in the United States' banking system

- Serving to balance the interest of the federal government, the interests of the banking system and the interests of consumers of the banking system

- Managing the nation's money supply in order to strike a balance of maximum employment, stable prices and moderate interest rates

- Providing financial services to foreign financial institutions, the United States government and the United States banking system, including the facilitation of payment between the regional Federal Reserve banks and responding to liquidity needs of the private banking system

During the recent Great Recession, the Federal Reserve along with the US Treasury department played and to a smaller degree are continuing to play significant roles in providing funds to the banking system and other private corporations to ensure the financial health of these institutions.

At this point in the history of the Federal Reserve, it is also fair to say that its problems are being increased as the federal government is running massive deficits to pay for wars in Iraq and Afghanistan, providing huge stimulus packages to prop up the economy and providing bailout funds to private banking and other huge private corporations. The success of the Federal Reserve to date in these troublesome times has been masterful, but whether good monetary policy can offset bad fiscal policy over the long term remains to be seen and is problematic.

Before doing some analysis of the problems confronting the Federal Reserve at the present time, we should assess its ability over its history and its role in transforming our nation.

In its early years during the boom period of the 1920's the Federal Reserve's monetary policy was somewhat expansionary. Some argue that it was too expansionary and helped cause the Great Depression. That may have been a factor but it certainly was not the only factor. Greed among many financial and other private institutions was a greater cause.

When the Great Depression occurred the Federal Reserve contracted the money supply. In doing that it has been accused of causing or extending the Great Depression. It again is debatable whether it caused the

Depression but it undoubtedly deserves some blame for not helping to stop or shorten it. The current Chairman of the Federal Reserve, Ben Bernanke, a student of the Great Depression, has acknowledged that the Federal Reserve's policy during that period did in fact serve to worsen the Depression.

There have been other periods of debate regarding the role of the Federal Reserve. After World War II, the debate was to what degree the Federal Reserve should monetize federal deficits. The monetization of the federal debt debate will be never ending because of the Federal Reserve's ability to expand or contract an "elastic" money supply.

In the 1970's the country was mired in an economic quagmire consisting of slow growth, high inflation, and high unemployment. The word "stagflation" was created to describe the period. The role of the Federal Reserve was again debated. In 1979, then President Carter nominated Paul Volcker as Chairman of the Federal Reserve. Volcker made some changes in the way the Federal Reserve viewed the money supply. He also began tightening the money supply and over the next few years inflation had decreased from double digit percentage increases to a modest one percent by early 1987.

In 1987, Alan Greenspan replaced Volcker as the Federal

Reserve Chairman. During Greenspan's lengthy tenure the United States' economy was generally healthy and Greenspan was given much credit for maintaining a sound monetary policy. Sound monetary policy helped maintain a good balance between growth, inflation and employment. During periods, when the stock market was making rapid gains, Greenspan coined the phrase, "irrational exuberance". With some 20/20 hindsight his words proved to be prophetic, and greed again would be a significant factor in the economic demise which occurred in 2008.

In February 2006 Ben Bernanke replaced Greenspan as Chairman of the Federal Reserve System. During his tenure he has been confronted with numerous challenges.

The Federal Reserve is an institution that is primarily a reactive organization. If the rest of the nation and world behaved economically, the job of the Fed would be far less difficult. It has been unfairly criticized for faults attributable to others, including the federal government and some of their poor fiscal policy decisions. It has also been necessary for the Fed to assume difficult situations due to poor behavior on the part of other financial institutions. It does have a reactive role and the way it reacts to situations can have a significant influence on the lives of all Americans.

The recent Great Recession was due to many of us. It was due to consumers who attempted to buy houses they could not afford. It was also due to consumers charging their credit cards for things they could not afford. It was due to financial institutions, which made terrible judgments on loans they granted to those who could not afford them. It was due to financial institutions that dabbled in financial instruments, they did not understand - that consumers did not understand - that financial regulators did not understand - and that politicians most assuredly did not understand.

Throughout the 1990's and the early part of the first decade of this millennium, the irrational exuberance described by Alan Greenspan was real. This nation was on a spending spree financed by debt at all levels. It was a period during which prices of housing became irrational and the value of stocks also became irrational in light of the huge indebtedness incurred by corporations, who were under the ever-illusionary belief that growth in quantity was more important than quality growth. It was a period during which local, state and federal governments incurred debt and spent at a more rapid pace than drunken sailors on a thirty-day pass. The balloon filled with huge pockets of debt was bound to eventually explode and explode it did.

The underlying culprit once again was greed and the desertion of "common sense" in making financial decisions at every level. Economic stability is dependent to some degree on the good moral judgment of citizens. Greed pollutes humans and it pollutes the economy. When the collective value system of a country deteriorates, the country also deteriorates in other ways.

We are now at the point that the federal government is becoming the borrower of last resort. During the Great Recession, the federal government began assuming the bad debts and bad decisions made by others in order to ward off financial panic. It is difficult to fault the federal government for the effort it made, but it made decisions that will have adverse long-term financial effects at almost all levels of American life. It will alter forever the relationship of government with the people and the free enterprise system.

The institution that is and will be greatly involved in the transformation of the American free enterprise system is the Federal Reserve. It has little choice but to be involved. Every reason for its existence will be a challenge for it in the foreseeable future.

The Fed has been an important player thus far in attempting to avoid financial panic during the Great Recession. In the spring of 2009, which was at the height of the Great Recession, the Federal Reserve released its balance sheet as of December 31, 2008. During 2008 the assets of the Federal Reserve almost doubled increasing from $1.33 trillion at 12/31/07 to $2.25 trillion at the end of 2008. The increase was attributable to loans to banks and other financial companies, a huge increase in central bank liquidity swaps and a large increase in investments held in various financing vehicles. Stated more simply, it has been through loans and assumptions of risks that the Federal Reserve has assumed the risk of many of the bad financial decisions and instruments made by inept and greedy "financiers".

The assets of the Federal Reserve continue to increase at a rapid rate. By the end of 2011 the assets had increased from the aforementioned $1.3 trillion at the end of 2007 to more than $2.9 trillion at that end of 2011.

The rapidly increasing federal debt during the past few years has led to the Federal Reserve increasing the money supply to help finance the debt. That is a new and high-risk endeavor given the huge amounts involved. It is a dangerous method of financing a portion of the federal debt, but it may have little choice. We are rapidly increasing our federal debt to levels that may lead to the inability of the federal government to sell its debt as it has done in the past. If and when that should happen dire results are very likely to follow.

In the short-term the role the Federal Reserve is playing may be of benefit but it may also be aiding in making the long-term problem of federal debt even greater than it otherwise would be.

As is true of the staggering indebtedness and unfunded liabilities of the Federal government, the average citizen may not understand the role the Federal Reserve is playing. By its ability to print money the Federal Reserve is effectively financing a portion of the US debt, thereby eliminating the need for the Federal government to issue a certain amount of debt instruments to other countries or institutions and also eliminating some interest expense.

It is somewhat parallel to a citizen printing money in his/her basement and thereby reducing their personal interest bearing debt. That average citizen would go to jail for what the Federal Reserve is doing. But the printing of money will eventually have severe consequences for the average citizen in the form of higher inflation.

In summary, the Federal Reserve and the federal government have assumed larger and larger amounts of risks that were made by bad decisions on the part of major banks, other financial institutions, and large corporations. In attempts to end the Great Recession the federal government has taken on commitments that will substantially increase the indebtedness of the federal government. The Federal Reserve may have to continue playing a major role in an attempt to maximize the monetization of the federal government debt. It will, for many years to come, walk the financial tightrope that balances inflation, growth and employment. It has a near impossible task in future years because there are limits to the degree it can provide assistance in financing the vast amount of federal deficits currently being incurred and which will be incurred into the foreseeable future.

Chapter 8 --- A Hybrid Economic System

At the present time a debate is taking place in this country regarding our economic system. Those who strongly favor a capitalistic system with less government intervention have concerns that we are drifting toward socialism. Those who want greater government control over the economic system deny that the country is moving toward socialism. Both sides are right to some degree and also wrong to some degree.

Capitalism or free enterprise system as envisioned by Adam Smith has come and gone in our country. It is true that we are still a country whose economic system is largely in the hands of private entrepreneurs or owned through corporations. However, the regulations and laws of state and federal governments are so extensive and intrusive that no private entrepreneurs or business corporations are truly free to produce as they wish. Our economic system has become a socially regulated economic system.

But, it is not true that we are a socialist country. Government ownership is not the norm although during the Great Recession the federal government took ownership positions in some large financial and a few non-financial corporations. However, the federal government claims that it is not the long-term intent of the federal government to maintain such ownership. That may be the intent and it does appear that the government will eliminate their ownership or control associated with the bailout of these large institutions. Whatever the future role of ownership may be, we can accurately state that our economic system is becoming more government controlled.

The words capitalism or socialism generally are not attuned to the economies existing in most countries in the world today. Even China's economy cannot be called a pure socialistic economy. The words "market socialist-oriented economy" are used to describe it and they call their own economy "socialism with Chinese characteristics". Most advanced economies of the world today fall somewhere between China and the United States. We are still a relatively free market oriented economy and China is a relatively controlled market oriented economy. What differentiates advanced economies is the degree of government control, along with social regulations and laws.

History is usually the best teacher of things that work

or don't work. Socialism to the extreme or communism has a poor track record. The economies of governments that ruled in the Soviet Union, China under Mao Zedong, and Cuba under Fidel Castro were economies that functioned poorly and governments that treated their entire society poorly. Those in power did not live poorly. While trumpeting equality for all, the leaders of those countries ruled the people and the economy with an iron hand. The "invisible hand" of Adam Smith gave way to the iron fist of the rulers. In the process of tight central control, incentives for the people were stifled. These countries, with the exception of Cuba, have turned toward some elements of free enterprise or capitalism.

The United States was and remains the best example of a free enterprise system. Nevertheless, it is not as free as it once was and to some degree that is appropriate due to tremendous growth in the economy and some obvious needs to ensure safe working conditions, environmental protection, minimum wages, etc. The debate in current times is not about some of these controls or government intervention, but rather how much control and government intervention. We do have a hybrid system containing both aspects of free enterprise and government control.

Government intervention in this country is not that new. In the latter part of the nineteenth century, as we became a more industrialized country, we also began seeing more corporations and trusts in our economic system. Some abuses by those enterprises called for government regulations, and reforms began being required by government. In the ensuing 150 years the trend line of government regulations and laws has moved steadily upward.

The question facing governments that wish to have the best economic system for their citizens is no longer a question of capitalism versus socialism, but how much government regulation and ownership is necessary to protect the social values of a country. At this point we can say that history tells us that communism or absolute socialism has not worked well. These governments have tended to become dictatorial and also take away the incentives that are part of the nature of free people. Big government can be as abusive of the rights of people or more so than big corporations. Power corrupts at the federal government level and therein is a real threat to the people of this country.

When people see abuses in our economic system they tend to vote for those promising an end to the abuses, but unfortunately the abuses are then all too frequently transferred from business to government. Two examples may help indicate this. In the early day of the Great Recession, corporate executives were criticized for flying to meetings in their corporate jets, but government officials do the same thing in government aircrafts. Private citizens are subject to fines and penalties when failing to properly report income on their tax returns. A number of candidates for high government office have been guilty of the same thing, but with far less outcry by government officials.

It is naïve to believe that big government can manage an economy better than it will be managed by free entrepreneurs, who have an economic interest in what and how they produce goods and services. Government officials do not have that economic interest. They simply ignore accountability and responsibility.

Why do people then vote for more government control? Self-interest is one answer and another likely answer is that they do not understand the long-term consequences of their vote. It is true that abuses occur in business and other aspects of our nation. They should be corrected. How to correct them is the real issue. More control by government may be an appropriate response in some cases. Safety, environmental protection, and certain financial regulations are three. But permanent control or ownership in some other areas is not the answer. Education, health care, and social security fall into that category.

Why does government seem to perpetually seek more intervention in the economic system? If Americans sincerely believe that it is a self-evident truth that all people are created equal and endowed by their Creator with the inalienable rights of life, liberty and the pursuit of happiness, it logically follows that the FREE enterprise system is the most desired economic system and the least government intervention required in that system is also the best socially regulated economic system. Many in this country believe that more and more government intervention is necessary or desirable. Since communism provides the ultimate amount of government invention, those who wish for more government also wittingly or unwittingly believe that communism would provide the best economic system.

We have already noted that the government of the countries in the Soviet Union did not provide either a free economic system or the best social system for people who naturally desire freedom. It is difficult to understand why people or government pursue a form of government that wishes to exert more control over an economic system than is required, when history has shown that such government is poor government and such economies are poor economies.

In an interview, Alan Greenspan, the former chairman of the Federal Reserve, made a very appropriate comment. When he was asked about the need for greater oversight and greater regulation, he gave an answer that was very much on point, but far too infrequently acknowledged by those in power. His simple and straightforward answer, which is a rarity for the former Chairman, was that regulations and laws do not exist that control the natural flaws of people. The job of government should be to understand the government role considering such flaws among men. That role was extremely well understood by our founding fathers. Government that governs least governs best. Our founding fathers had a great collective moral philosophy as well as a great collective political philosophy.

As the industrial revolution began in this country, those who led and managed trusts, corporations and monopolies took advantage of workers and consequently government enacted reforms. In the boom period of the 1920's the opportunity for greater and greater profits by too many financial and corporate leaders, led to abuses and the Great Depression and more laws and regulations came into being. During the boom period of the 1990's and early 2000's abuses and greed led to excesses and once again government has stepped in with more laws, and more bailouts for those who really don't deserve bailouts.

Government is guilty of deception when it promises what it can't deliver. It has assumed some financial and other risks once assumed by individuals and corporations which were excessive and in the process it has overtaxed the people who don't deserve the tax and taken on debt that must be paid by future generations.

In regards to both our economic and governmental systems, both have failed us when excesses and greed have crept into the picture. When President Washington left office over 200 years ago he made the two previously noted observations. One was that virtue or morality is the springboard to popular government. The other was that history and experience teach us that a national morality cannot prevail in the absence of religious principle (faith-based morality). Faith-based morality is important in all aspects of individual lives, communities and government. It is also a necessity for success in an economic system. Greed and lust for power and excessive income and profits have been the real culprits that have led to the need for government intervention.

Despite all its flaws the economic system of the United States is still the best economic system existing in the world today. As noted earlier the words capitalism and socialism no longer apply and create meaningless and bitter partisan rhetoric. Our hybrid free enterprise system with government regulations and laws to ensure the social welfare of all citizens is still the best economic model in the world today. The debate of the degree of free enterprise versus the amount of necessary government control is an appropriate debate. If history has taught us anything it is that we should err on the side of maximizing freedom within the economic system.

Economic systems do not exist in a vacuum. They are part of the culture of a nation and that culture is part of the moral values of a country. The importance of faith-based morality that George Washington and the other founding fathers philosophically understood has not changed. The complexities of economies and cultures have changed but the nature of people has not changed and people have a strong desire for freedom. Our founding fathers understood that and put a government in place to provide such freedom.

People are also driven strongly by faith or lack thereof and our founding fathers also understood that. People are not necessarily driven by religious affiliation but rather by faith. Some have faith in a Creator, God, Allah or a series of gods and in a life after death. Others have the belief that no God or gods exist and that there is no life after death. That too is a form of faith (or anti-faith) inasmuch as it too is a belief that cannot be proven.

It has been stated and I concur that not all religious people are good people and that not all good people are religious people. But it is my belief, which was also the belief of our founding fathers, that it is a kind and merciful God that endows human beings with inalienable rights.

Faith in a kind and merciful supernatural God and life hereafter do lead to goodness in people. The love for others and belief that all people are created equal and all would like to be treated as we ourselves wish to be treated are the true signs of the goodness of people, the goodness of cultures, the goodness of economic systems and the goodness of governments. The rest of this book will be dedicated to the linkage of faith and morals, cultural values and economics and how they have all played a role in the transformation of our nation.

Chapter 9 --- The Changing American Dream

The words "American Dream" are often used to describe the pursuit and fulfillment of the inalienable right to happiness. Before we examine how that dream is pursued and fulfilled, it would be good to have a definition. Unfortunately, that is not possible because the American Dream has a special and individual meaning to every American. Each of us has our own view of the American Dream.

The opening two sentences of the Declaration of Independence best defined that which make a good nation and also permit every human being the right to pursue the American Dream. The first sentence states the importance of natural law in the role of human beings. The second sentence regarding self-evident truths best summarizes the value system that can provide the American Dream. Both sentences are noted early in the first chapter of this book. If our country ever ignores the value system established by our founding fathers in those first two sentences of the Declaration it will be a colossal error.

Those opening words of the Declaration of Independence best describe the rights of citizens and the purpose of government. In my earlier books, much space was devoted to the importance of the inalienable rights of life and liberty. Much of the remainder of this chapter will be devoted to the pursuit of happiness and the common threads of the fabric of our society that lead to such happiness.

Is the pursuit of happiness best fulfilled by material desires, spiritual desires or other goals?

At the end of the prior chapter, it was noted that faith is a strong motivational force in people. Our founding fathers recognized that force. Our founding fathers were not only great leaders; they had a great understanding of moral and human philosophy. Their philosophical views on people and what drives people were major considerations for the country they helped create.

In chapter 5, the progression of a democracy from our alleged friend, Professor Tyler, was noted. The progression was from bondage to spiritual faith, and then progressed to great courage, liberty, abundance, selfishness, complacency, apathy, dependency and then back to bondage.

It is noteworthy that those released from bondage first progressed to spiritual faith. In that part of the progression, I concur with the Professor. History reinforces that progression as witnessed by the Biblical story of Exodus, the turning to faith of the people of Europe after bondage, and the spiritual faith of many who were slaves in this country. However the progression of democracy continues on to abundance and selfishness. History also supports that contention.

Many people do have a spiritual desire as well as the desire for material things. Both become incorporated into the pursuit of happiness and The American Dream.

Before people can pursue happiness they must first have the inalienable right to life and freedom fulfilled. Then they can pursue happiness as they wish to define happiness. Yes, our founding fathers had it sequentially correct.

Freedom is the key to the pursuit of happiness. Freedom also means the right to pursue abundance, selfishness, complacency, apathy and dependency. In summary freedom gives everyone the right to pursue happiness as they wish to define happiness and therein lies the strength of this nation. Therein may also lie the demise of this nation.

The inalienable right to the pursuit of happiness demands recognition of two strong traits of people. One is the motivational trait of faith and the other is freedom. Faith is that mysterious trait in humans that accounts for goodness within humans but has also been falsely blamed for evil. Far too many wars have been due to excesses incorrectly attributed to faith. Flaws in humans that are also wrongly attributed to faith are the cause of too much strife among humans. Faith includes the belief in supernatural powers and a flawed view of faith (or anti-faith) disavows the supernatural. As long as faith does not lead to the intervention in the freedom of others it needs to be recognized by government as it was by the founding fathers. They recognized that it was appropriate for faith to be practiced through religions, and they also recognized that government should not endorse specific religions nor should government prohibit them. It should be no surprise that freedom of religion and freedom of speech are part of the first amendment of our Constitution.

While writing this chapter I asked a number of relatives and friends to define the pursuit of happiness and when such happiness was accomplished. Some stated love and the need to be loved; some noted a sense of purpose or accomplishment. Most stated the right to pursue their faith and thereby achieve ultimate happiness in heaven. Most also stated the right to pursue necessary material needs. The definition of the pursuit of happiness in our country covers a wide spectrum of views. None of the views expressed, noted concerns that freedom in this country was restrictive to their right to pursue happiness. At this point, it seems that most of us are satisfied that we still have the necessary freedom to pursue happiness and that is important. It is that right that government can provide. The fulfillment is up to the individual.

Freedom to pursue material wealth is also a strong motivating force of people, but just as excesses of flawed faith have led to abuses so has the excessive pursuit of material wealth. These flaws in human beings need to be recognized by government if government does the best job of governing. What helped make this country great was that our founding fathers recognized both the good and evil in humans. People will not have the right to pursue happiness if they cannot express their faith and they will not have the right to happiness if they cannot pursue material wealth, even to the point of excess. But once people have the rights to pursue both, government must also understand that humans will abuse the privilege of these freedoms and so we must have laws and regulations.

Spiritual faith, when properly understood, can and does lead to the best values among people. Faithful people belong to many different religions and some do not belong to any religion. Many studies have linked faithful and religious people to happiness. One belief among most major religions is that human kindness is the most important trait humans possess in their relationship with each other. It is secondary only to the love of our Creator. When we truly believe that all other humans are as good as we are and that they deserve the same love and respect we want, we have the best conditions achievable while we live on this earth.

Unfortunately, the trait of humans to pursue material wealth too often clashes with the love of neighbor. At some point the pursuit of material wealth can result in greed and greed can override the love of neighbor. It is fair to conclude that when we have the optimal love of neighbor we also have the best society on earth and when greed prevails we have the worst society. So how are we as a nation doing?

Historically the pursuit of the American Dream included the right to pursue our spiritual goals and the financial resources to have enough food on the table, a roof over our head, a means of transportation, a vacation and time for entertainment or entertaining activities. Greed gets into the equation when we want more of these than we need or which others possess.

As noted in the beginning of this chapter, it is impossible for any one person to define the pursuit of happiness or the American Dream for another person. The pursuit of happiness it too individualistic to permit a definition to cover everyone.

My personal pursuit of happiness relates very much to my faith and my Christian beliefs. It is my belief that "Heaven" will be the ultimate happiness for me and for others. In pursuing that goal it is my belief that my personal pursuit of happiness comes from living a life on earth that will result in reaching Heaven.

It is also my belief that living a moral life pursuant to my views of a faith-based morality is the best way for me and for others to pursue happiness on earth.

But morality cannot be dictated for anyone other than myself. Therefore, my own beliefs must incorporate the respect for the beliefs of others, because one of my personal beliefs is that the pursuit of happiness requires me to love my neighbor as myself. That in turn means respecting their views as I respect my own views.

My own views of how to live a faith-based morality are incorporated in the two commandments given us by the person I consider the greatest moral philosopher to walk this earth, i.e. Jesus Christ. The two commandments are to love God above all else and to love my neighbor as myself. If everyone truly followed those commands life on earth would more closely parallel life in Heaven.

But other people's view of the pursuit of happiness is different than mine and to have a peaceful earth we need to respect the views of others.

As we have become a more affluent society the pursuit of happiness has gone through some transformation. Polls indicate that a larger percentage of citizens now see the pursuit of happiness being satisfied more by material wants than by spiritual wants.

As noted earlier, we cannot define the American Dream or pursuit of happiness for others but we can make some judgments from observations and polls. Polls do indicate that the percentage of people who eschew religion and/ or faith has grown in recent years.

By observation we see that in our modern society we have built larger homes than ever before. We drive larger cars and have more material goods than did our forefathers. Polls also indicate that material wealth does not increase happiness and thus the pursuit of happiness from material things may be a futile pursuit.

The pursuit of happiness may have been transformed to some degree, but there is no indication or polling data suggesting that the pursuit of material goods provides greater happiness than the pursuit of spiritual goals.

In the pursuit of material wealth we have become

more indebted as consumers. In attempts to satisfy the increasing desires of the American people, local, state and federal government have become more indebted and governments at all levels tax citizens at high rates.

We have already indicated the result of higher taxes and higher debt. In the attempt to satisfy our ever increasing appetite for material things we have placed a mortgage on future generations. It is not just government that is to blame. It is also we the people.

We think we are a more enlightened society today, but our values of today are also flawed. Love of God, love of neighbor and love of "self evident" truths are too easily set aside. Some call it political correctness, some call it secular rights but when any rights violate the faith-based moral right that we love God and love our neighbor as our self we have values that detract from my perception of the American dream.

We now have the government-sanctioned right to kill human beings via abortion. Too many Americans have learned to accept that. History should have taught us that every time we decide to classify a human being as a non-person we have gotten it wrong. At the highest level of government and our judicial system we have at one time or another classified African Americans, Native Americans and Japanese Americans as not having the equal rights granted other Americans. Today, we take away that right from the unborn. Too many Americans accept that the unborn do not have the right to the American Dream.

Too many Americans accept the breakdown of the nuclear family. We now have over 40 percent of our children born to unmarried women. Too many of us accept that and ignore that those children have an impediment to live the American dream. They will not be given the loving nuclear family environment that provides the mercy of a mother and the justice of a father.

Government and education have become partners in the refusal to teach faith-based morals to our children. Too many Americans accept that.

Government and especially the judicial system now proclaim many rights that damage the general welfare of the nation. Too many Americans accept that. We have many rights but should not have a right that is damaging to others and therefore does not further the general welfare of this nation.

Instead of encouraging prayer in the public school classrooms for all religions of the world, we prohibit it for all. Too many Americans accept that.

Yes, the American Dream has changed. George

Washington understood the danger of evolving too far down the road of secular morality when he warned us that reason and experience should be a lesson that a national or faith-based morality can be lost without certain faith-based principles.

When we begin losing faith-based principles, other principles that are secular and tend to evolve, replace the faith-based principles. Lust of power, greed, and materialistic desires replace the simple faith and the American Dream of our forefathers.

Chapter 10 --- The New Social Order

In the progression through the early stages of a democracy our alleged friend, Professor Tyler, noted the traits of spiritual faith, courage and liberty before abundance. After abundance he noted selfishness, complacency apathy and dependency. I am not sure that these traits apply to a majority of individuals in this nation, but there seems to be some truth in his progression to the collective traits of this nation.

My own view would be that the dominant characteristic of the nation in its early years was the dedication to a faith-based morality and more recently to a secular-based morality. A faith-based morality is characterized by faith and love of a Creator and a love of neighbor. The preamble to our Declaration of Independence was based on such a morality.

Secular morality has no foundation of firm beliefs. Such morality shifts as human beliefs and human leaders' beliefs shift. That morality has shifted substantially since the founding of this nation. Secular humanism may best describe some of the changes in secular morality.

The Council for Secular Humanism states, "secular humanists accept a world view or philosophy called naturalism, in which the physical laws of the universe are not superseded by non-material or supernatural entities". They acknowledge that they are generally nontheists. They do not rely upon a God to solve their problems or PROVIDE GUIDANCE FOR THEIR CONDUCT.

Before discussing the type of morality which is most beneficial to a society, I have noted that it is my belief that not all good people belong to a religion nor are all people who claim a religion good people. I also believe that many who adopt secular-based morality do not proclaim to be secular humanists. Many people believe in aspects of both faith-based morality and secular-based morality. A recently deceased friend of mine claimed that agnosticism best described his spiritual beliefs but at the same time he believed in the morality that flows from the Ten Commandments.

This much is clear. Although the founding fathers believed and noted in the Constitution that religion and government should not be intertwined they most assuredly believed that a faith-based morality was the best morality for a nation. It is why I often make reference to the two statements from President Washington's farewell address. He noted, "Virtue or morality is the springboard to popular government".

He also noted that "Reason and experience forbid us to expect that national morality can prevail in exclusion of religious principle", which I refer to as faith-based morality.

Faith-based morality was the predominant morality of this nation for the first 175 plus years of its existence. In the past fifty to sixty years many have adopted more and more of the morality of secular humanism. There are virtually no boundaries of behavior for secular humanism. It vacillates with the humanistic views of people. There is no foundation on which it is based. For thousands of years it was accepted that marriage was between a man and a woman. My Webster dictionary still defines marriage as a relationship between a man and woman. As this is being written a number of states now permit the marriage of men to men and women to women. Faith-based morality makes that unacceptable. Secular morality makes it acceptable.

Secular morality is not related only to current times. I am a great admirer of our founding fathers, but they too had their flaws. Some were slave owners and that could only be justified by a secular moral viewpoint. It was against the basic faith-based belief that all people are created equal and possess an inalienable right to freedom.

The Supreme Court judges of this country also justified

slavery on the secular and narrow definition that slaves were not citizens. They did that in Scott versus Sanford. Judges too sometimes forget or ignore our inalienable rights, which should transcend secular rights.

The treatment of many Native Americans could only be justified from a secular-based moral viewpoint. Faith-based morality should have dictated equality and their inalienable right to freedom for all African and Native Americans.

Those and other historical evils could only be justified from a secular morality point of view. As noted earlier there is no foundation upon which secular morality is based.

Reason and experience as President Washington noted would dictate that a faith-based morality also provides the best national morality. The United States blazed a moral trail in adopting a faith-based morality. No country is perfect because it is made up of human beings who are flawed, but faith-based morality provides the beliefs and foundation that provide the best moral code for a nation. This nation has had social injustices throughout its history, but on balance it has been a good and noble nation.

In our more recent history, our country has begun deviating more and more from faith-based morality and too frequently has justified social behavior based on secular-based morality. The ideals of secular humanism are becoming more prevalent and less reliance is placed on our Creator as the guide for proper conduct. That has created a shift in the social priorities and the social order of our nation.

Societies change through the course of history and our society has been transformed, especially in the past sixty years. There is some good news. As a nation we have truly become a melting pot of many different ethnic backgrounds. The assimilation and acceptance of these diverse backgrounds is one of the strengths of our nation. Much of the progress in better human relations has occurred in the past sixty years.

Good news does not exist for many of the other cultural changes in our society. The justification for abortions can only be rationalized by leaning on secular humanism as justification and by parsing the words of our Constitution. Every time this nation has denied the rights of personhood to a human being it has been wrong. That was true of slavery - true of the treatment of Native Americans- true of the unequal treatment of women - true of the treatment of Japanese Americans during World War II and true of the aborted unborn. Abortions simply stated are sanctioned murder of unborn HUMAN BEINGS. Euthanasia and the death penalty also can only be justified from a secular-based view of morality, although the latter is somewhat debatable.

If you want an example of the contrast in our society in the past sixty years, look at the average movie filmed in the 1950's and compare it to the average movie of today. Foul language was taboo in the films of the fifties; modest dress was demanded and the total absorption with sex was not that prevalent. I did not and do not look to Hollywood for any moral leadership, but in the 1950's it was constrained by the faith-based morals still dominating our society at that time period.

In the 1950's the definition of marriage remained the same as it had been for thousands of years. It was a God-blessed bond between a man and woman. That is the faith-based definition of marriage. But that very basic and long-term definition is being eroded. As noted earlier it is now recognized in several states as a bond that can extend to two men or two women. Based on secular humanism that definition could be extended to a number of men and a number of women or it could be extended to include an animal and a human. There are no boundaries for secular-based morality. What was unthinkable sixty years ago has become reality today and pursuant to the beliefs of secular humanists, what is unacceptable today may be acceptable in another fifty years. Secular humanistic beliefs are changing the very basic structure of American society.

The breakdown in the family has also led to a high percentage of children being born to unwed mothers. That too is okay under the rules of secular humanism, because God is not involved in the guidance of secular-based morality. The number of children being raised in non-nuclear family settings is increasing.

The sanctity of life and the sanctity of marriage under the moral guidance of faith have changed society in this nation. There simply is no foundation to provide guidance for moral behavior when faith-based morality is taken out of the picture.

Where secular-morality will lead us is anyone's guess. Moral codes that have long been in existence and derived from the "self-evident belief" that they are provided by our Creator are eroding.

When those beliefs erode, human behavior tends to deteriorate. If there is no guidance from God, then power, greed, material goods and other flaws of humans, become acceptable and often are the measurements of success. We are only beginning to emerge from a Great Recession that was partially and maybe primarily due to greed.

If humans begin believing that there are no boundaries that constitute acceptable behavior then traditional boundaries erode. Society changes and in this country society is changing. If fulfillment comes from drugs do drugs.

The culture of a society is dependent on the morals of a society. They are linked. Eventually the culture and morals also affect the economics of a society. Power becomes a driving force in a faith-based moral vacuum. Self-fulfillment replaces faith.

We are becoming governed by some people who believe they have a birthright to hold office.

Much of the daily activities of politicians are now devoted to perpetuating themselves in office rather than spending their time doing the will of the people.

Corporate executives, who are void of a faith-based conscience, find it acceptable to take millions of dollars in compensation.

The news media find satisfaction in presenting partisan viewpoints instead of providing objective news.

Kindness to fellow humans may or may not be a motivating force in a secular humanistic society.

The general welfare stated in the Preamble to the Constitution becomes secondary to the fulfillment of materialistic desires. Materialism provides the greatest source of satisfaction to those living according to secular humanistic standards. Faith has no role.

Sexual appetites are fulfilled within or without marriage. Sexual desires are filled at younger and younger ages. Traditional boundaries regarding sex have eroded.

So in our society today we do have a new social order. We sanction murder of the unborn. We devalue marriage. We find fulfillment in materialism. We find satisfaction in drugs. We find satisfaction without limits in sex. Greed makes sense. Power is the fulfillment of secular morality. Getting to heaven is the quirky belief of those who cling to faith-based morality. Secular humanism is becoming more of a standard and replacing faith-based behavior. We are losing sight of why we became a nation

I wish that my views were written hyperbole. Sadly they are not. We have indeed created a new social order. Morality without a foundation is not a lasting morality.

People living a true faith-based morality understand that it is in this life that we pursue happiness by living a life of goodness through which we will find eternal happiness in life after death. It is not surprising that polls indicate religious people to be the happiest people.

They better understand that happiness is the result of a faithful life.

We have been given the perfect blueprint and the perfect plan of action that did and still can provide the most desirable society. The greatest moral philosopher who walked on this earth gave them to us. Love God above all else and your neighbor as yourself. To love God above all else means to love and follow those two commands he gave us. Thomas Jefferson who did not claim any specific religion affiliation agreed with the philosophy of the greatest moral philosopher. The flawed nature of human beings never permits the fulfillment of the ideal society, which total compliance with Christ's two commands would provide. No matter what a person's religion affiliation, there have not been two commands that would better provide the ideal society if those commands were followed.

People debase religion and they defile God because they can point to evil behavior of humans who proclaim to be religious. But no one can point to anything that would provide a better society than living according to the commands He gave us. The more we drift from those two commands the more we drift from the best social order people can have. Our founding fathers understood that.

Despite the turn toward secular humanistic values by

too many, their views and beliefs do not, at least as yet, represent the beliefs of a majority of Americans. Polls continue to indicate that to be the case. A recent poll also indicated that a majority of Americans pray daily. Hopefully, they occasionally say a prayer that this country will adhere to a faith-based morality. We have already proceeded too far down the path of secular-based morality.

Chapter 11 --- The New Economic Order

$\mathcal{J}$t would be interesting to have our founding fathers and their political philosophies with us in the world we live in today. Would their views on freedom or liberty change due to the complexities of our current and more complex nation or would they adhere to their cherished views of what makes a great nation? Jefferson could surely boast that he was prophetic when he said that the natural progress of things is for liberty to yield and government to gain ground. His comment has become true for us as individuals and it is also true for our free enterprise system.

In earlier chapters we have defined the ways in which government has become more and more involved in the free enterprise system. In the late 19th century, as trusts and corporations were formed, the intervention of government began to accelerate. The period following the Great Depression brought on substantial increases in government involvement in the economy and the rate of increase has continued to the current time.

This country's citizens are divided between those who wish to see a reduction in government intervention and those who seek a larger role for government. Our political parties differ on the issue as well, but regardless of which party is in office government continues to grow. Regulations increase and laws multiply.

Despite the increase in regulations and laws, there are some things that cannot be done by legislation and government intervention. Government cannot legislate faith or morality. Government cannot legislate human kindness. Government cannot legislate initiative and the willingness to work hard. Government cannot legislate away the flaws of human beings.

In 1916, William Boetcker, a Presbyterian minister, authored a pamphlet entitled, "The Ten Cannots". The ten cannots are often erroneously attributed to Abraham Lincoln. But since they deal with human nature as well as economic and human values they are worth noting:

You cannot bring about prosperity by discouraging thrift.

You cannot strengthen the weak by weakening the strong.

You cannot help little men by tearing down big men.

You cannot lift the wage earner by pulling down the wage payer.

You cannot help the poor by destroying the rich.

You cannot establish sound security on borrowed money.

You cannot further the brotherhood of man by encouraging class hatred.

You cannot keep out of trouble by spending more than you earn.

You cannot build character and courage by taking away man's initiative and independence.

You cannot help men permanently by doing for them what they could and should do for themselves.

One can agree or disagree with any or all of the above but before government intervenes too frequently in the affairs of its citizens it would be well served to occasionally give some consideration to the above.

One of the problems with communism, the ultimate form of socialism, was that it believed it could make cans out of the aforementioned cannots. Soviet Union countries, Cuba and China, before moving away somewhat from a pure socialistic system, are evidence of the failure of centrally run and centrally owned government economies. But why is that the case?

Prosperity and the pursuit of happiness requires freedom. As government becomes larger, liberties diminish as noted by Jefferson. When liberties diminish incentives for the people and for entrepreneurs also diminish and the productivity of a nation begins to decline. I think Jefferson would concur with that analysis. In light of our diminished liberty, let us examine the economic situation in our nation today and also evaluate the causes that have brought about the current economic environment.

In a democracy or republic the people are to some degree responsible for change. They vote for those in power. When candidates promise better things and voters are convinced that they will deliver, they tend to vote for the candidate who promises more. It is a basic flaw in the thinking of many citizens that government can do something for less money than the free enterprise system. As government tries to provide more it merely increases the taxes and borrows the money to deliver on the promises made. In the process that which is delivered ultimately comes at a higher cost to the taxpayer due to the additional costs of government which are required to deliver on their promises. Cost efficiencies are not as important to government as they are to private entrepreneurs. Government does not have a profit motive. When there is no profit motive, the incentive for efficiency is lost.

Earlier in this book we indicated four factors that have greatly impacted the federal government. They were taxes, federal debt, social security and health care for senior citizens (Medicare).

The United States is already a heavily taxed nation. Its citizens not only pay federal income taxes but most also pay state income taxes. They also pay county and local taxes in the form of real property taxes, and personal property taxes in addition to FICA taxes, Medicare taxes, sales taxes, gas taxes, luxury taxes, alcohol taxes, cigarette taxes and a variety of other taxes. At the margin all forms of taxes now require more than 40% of the earnings of a middle class family in many states.

If the middle class and wealthier are forced to pay more taxes in the future than they currently do, the money needed for economic growth will be transferred to the government. But without tax increases there is little hope of decreasing the federal debt, as interest costs will make deficits larger in the future even if other programs are not increased. It will be difficult for the economy to grow fast enough to generate the increases in revenues necessary to cover the increases in the federal debt.

Income taxes were not a major issue in this nation for the first 150 years. But following World War I they have become a big, big factor. A significant downside of the taxes is that they are corrupting politicians. The power Washington now possesses is a huge problem. To manage a government that spends more than $3.5 trillion a year is simply not doable and accountability is lacking. Waste becomes larger and even the good programs become poorly administered. Worst of all, liberties diminish as government grows.

In the absence of a revolution, there seems to be no limit to the continuing growth of government. And with the continuing growth of government it is likely that taxes at their current level or higher will be a necessary part of life for our generation and many generations to follow. As noted earlier, even with no increase in programs, the deficit due to interest payments will grow and that means increases in taxes, or increases in the national debt or both.

In the chapter on federal debt we noted that it could easily reach or exceed $20 trillion in another five years and the annual interest payment on the debt at that time assuming a 5 percent rate would be a trillion dollars. As was also noted that alone would require each citizen to pay $3,000 per year in taxes or $12,000 for a family of four. Remember, that is just the amount to cover the cost of interest expense on the national debt for one year.

In previous chapters I have also noted that the Social Security System could be improved if it were administered by a non-government entity. Let me demonstrate by using a simple example which utilizes the current FICA rates and current dollars. Let's assume a person is age 22 and works to age 67 and during those 45 years earns an average of $50,000 per year. If the employee and employer's contribution were placed into a fund earning 4 % yearly, the amount in the fund would at age 67 equal $750,000. Assuming the fund continued to earn 4 % during retirement that person could withdraw $30,000 per year and still have the $750,000 remaining in his/her estate at the time of death. Government could have done that and could still do that and guarantee those payments via ERISA as is done with private pension funds.

At the present time the Social Security System and the Medicare System are substantially underfunded. Combined, the underfunding depending on the assumptions used, is somewhere in the range of $120 trillion. As noted earlier in this book that would be another assessment of about $380,000 for every citizen or about $1,500,000 for a family of four.

If we have not yet convinced you that you are slowly becoming subservient to the power of big government we probably never will. As government grows your liberties diminish, and the more you look to government the more they will continue to diminish.

This chapter was supposed to deal with this country's new economic order. So why spend as much time as I have on government? The answer is that government is now not just a player in our economy but is the substantial player in our economic system. In recent years it has become an even bigger player. As noted many times we have a socially regulated economic system, and government has indicated it is willing to become a stockholder of some of our major corporations.

Our financial community will be more regulated than in the past. Their recent obsession with bigness was somewhat to blame as was their inability to assess the reasonable amount of risk they could assume. Their actions led to greater government involvement and they along with the rest of us will probably have to live with substantially greater government financial regulations in the future.

The automobile industry in this country too will be a changed industry. Government is somewhat to blame for their failures during the Great Recession because of costly regulations and costly demands. The industry was not blameless and their labor union, the UAW, also shares blame. The automobile industry was subjected to partial ownership by the federal government and is subjected to extensive regulations.

Too many corporations believe that bigger is better and

that is faulty thinking. In the pursuit of bigness without purpose, many of our major corporations have been managed poorly and in the process became subjects of bigger government.

The health care industry is also headed for greater government involvement. That too will not be good for average Americans. If people of the country don't express concerns to government to leave most of the health care industry in private hands, they will probably unwittingly also be asking for health care rationing as other countries with socialized medicine have experienced.

The energy business has been subject to big government regulations for a number of years. It will become even more so as the need for energy grows and the demand for cleaner energy also grows. We are also relying more on imported energy. With large supply of resources available that need not be the case, but government is largely to blame for dependency on foreign sources.

Governmental environmental controls have been extensive and now are also affecting the farming business. Environmental concerns related to the protection of threatened and endangered species are beginning to cause a decline in the necessary food supply of the nation and we are becoming more dependent on imported food.

The transportation industry, including airlines, rail transportation, trucking transportation and more recently automobiles are subject to ever increasing government regulation.

In other industries government regulations and taxes add to the cost of producing goods and services in this nation. No relief is in sight.

Despite all the concerns noted, this nation is still the major economy in the world today, but that is changing. It is so significantly larger that it will likely be many years before any other nation replaces us as the major economic nation in the world. However, a big problem is the high levels of consumer, corporate and government debt which continue to diminish this nation's economic advantage. Reestablishing creditworthiness at every level of our economy along with the difficulty of government's ability to borrow will have long-term negative impact on our economy. That is happening.

We are now emerging from a severe recession for which excesses in debt at every level of the economy were somewhat to blame. In the process of helping to reestablish growth in the economy, stability in the financial and automobile businesses, and help employment, the federal government has committed itself to ever increasing amounts of federal indebtedness.

We are fortunate that we are still a democratic republic. We the people still vote for our representatives in Washington and we also vote in primaries. We vote on bond issues. We have voted for those who are a big part of the problem. Yes, Professor Tyler we have experienced abundance and in our greed have sought more, and what we have sought more of we are receiving along with the higher taxes and debt required to pay for those wants. In our greed, we have shown little concern for those who are to come after us.

Another quote from Thomas Jefferson can be expanded today. Jefferson stated, "When we are directed from Washington when to sow and when to reap we will soon want bread". When in the economy of today we seek help we shall soon have higher taxes and more help than we would like.

Chapter 12 --- The Future of America

It is a difficult and somewhat futile to attempt to predict the future course of a nation, but we will try. In making such an attempt, history often provides the best indicator of what to expect in the future. In this book and previous books I have frequently repeated a quote from our first President. In his farewell address, George Washington noted that history and experience forbid us to believe that a national morality can prevail in the absence of religious principle, which I refer to as a national faith-based morality.

The national morality of a nation is important to its future. It is also my belief that a faith-based morality needs to be distinguished from a religion-based morality and a purely secular-based morality. Those distinctions have been made in this book and in my prior books.

As just noted, it is my view that this nation's future is somewhat dependent on the morality it chooses as a national morality. It is a choice of society, because government in a democracy tends to follow the wishes of a society. Our national faith-based morality is distinguished in three ways - the collective belief in a supernatural Creator - the collective belief that we should love our neighbor as yourself - the collective belief that hard work and sacrifice are necessary to build a better life for us and for our society. Without those values a nation tends to drift through a series of secular based values. At the beginning of Chapter 5, I used a quotation from an alleged Professor Alexander Tyler to indicate his belief of the series of values through which a democratic society progresses.

This book also devotes a number of chapters to our economic system and the changes through which it has evolved to the present time. That economic evolution has something to do with the third value I attribute to faith-based morality, which is hard work and sacrifice.

There is much good news in viewing the future of this nation. We are still largely a nation, in which the majority of people remain adherents of a national faith-based morality. We are still a nation that largely believes that our hard work and sacrifices for the benefit of our generation and future generations build a better life and a better nation. The problem with our nation is that too many have begun abandoning these core values and that includes too many who are a part of government and help determine this nation's future path.

For many generations this nation endorsed the moral

philosophy of our founding fathers and thus embraced a faith-based morality. We are a nation which has digressed further and further away from that national morality noted by Washington, and endorsed by our other founding fathers. How does moving away from the principles endorsed by our founding fathers, affect us today?

Let us first begin with the economy. We have already noted that income taxes, the federal debt, and the unfunded liabilities of Social Security and Medicare present serious economic problems for this nation and will have a serious consequence on the future citizens of our nation. The selfishness and greed of current and recent generations, together with the decisions of government, will become the burden of future generations.

It has also been noted that an American middle class family pays a large percentage of its earning to government at the local, state and federal level plus payroll and other taxes. That level of taxation will have to continue into future generations because our federal debt continues to grow and even if no more programs were added (highly unlikely) taxation must be continued at the current high or even higher levels just to continue servicing the interest on the increased debt. The payment of interest by future generations will not provide them with any benefits.

High taxation takes away some percentage of the capital needed for economic growth. Alan Greenspan, our former Federal Reserve Chairman, put it well when he said that taxation is a drag on economic growth and how much of a drag, is simply a matter of the degree of taxation. Taxation also discourages incentive and initiative and in the process encourages apathy. You cannot help the wage earner by pulling down the wage payer and taxation pulls down the wage payer.

Our high levels of taxation will be a drag on economic growth for many generations to come.

Federal debt too will be a drag on future economic growth because it has reached dangerous levels. One result is that of ensuring high taxation in the future which has already been noted. But other dangers to the economy due to high levels of debt also will be a problem. At some point it will become more difficult for this nation to sell its debt to others. At some point in the future, it would not be a surprise to this writer if the auctions of Treasury bonds, notes and bills become a newsworthy and nerve-wracking event in this country. China has already indicated its dissatisfaction with our high levels of debt and our budgets which forecast even higher levels of debt going into the future.

It is difficult to predict what may happen if the sale of federal debt becomes a problem. At the present time many financial transactions around the world are settled based on the currency of the United States. A failure in the sale of US debt would have serious world-wide repercussions. It would have a devastating effect on our economy for generations to come. It would force a financial discipline never before experienced by this nation.

Even if a financial catastrophe can be avoided, higher levels of debt in the future will further damage the creditworthiness of Treasury bonds, notes and bills. As creditworthiness is damaged, interest rates on debt will increase in order to encourage other nations and financial institutions to continue buying our federal debt. That is a simple economics. As the risk of indebtedness increases so does the cost of indebtedness. The FEDERAL GOVERNMENT IS NOT IMMUNE from credit problems.

High levels of indebtedness, in all likelihood, will also contribute to higher future levels of inflation. As we increase indebtedness we will probably have to increase the money supply. In many ways increased indebtedness is a proxy for an increase in the money supply if the indebtedness does not add to productivity. Attempts will be made to monetize the debt. Those increases in the money supply along with the non-productive increase in the federal debt will not necessarily help economic growth and as the money supply and debt increase faster than growth, inflation too will increase. That too is simple economics.

Our high levels of taxation and high levels of debt will be a drag on economic growth for many generations and will also lead to higher average inflation than has been experienced in recent years.

A potential scenario for the future is that this nation will again experience stagflation as it did in the 1970's, when slow growth was accompanied by high inflation, high interest rates and high unemployment. Slow growth and high unemployment have already become a reality.

For the past twenty five-years much of the economic growth of the country has been due to the ever increasing levels of debt by the consumer, by local and state governments via bonds issues, by corporations and finally by the federal government. Our recent Great Recession was in large part due to those high and irresponsible levels of debt. In order to provide bailouts and stimulus packages to consumers, state and local governments and large corporations, the federal government incurred staggering amounts of debt, which will further weaken and damage its creditworthiness. Rating agencies have become concerned with the creditworthiness of the federal debt obligations.

In addition to the problems of high taxation and high

levels of debt, this nation has unsustainable levels of unfunded liabilities attributable to Social Security, Medicare and Medicaid. The day is rapidly approaching when payments for entitlement programs will exceed revenues and therefore some action is likely within the next few years. No doubt the government, as it normally does, will increase taxation, but it may also have to curtail the current levels of increases in Social Security and probably force people to reach an older age before they can collect benefits from Social Security. It is also likely that fixing Medicare and our broader health system will entail some forms of rationing of health care. Hopefully, future reforms will include the involvement of the private sector as discussed in earlier chapters.

Increasing the federal income tax rates is not the only way to increase taxation. That can happen via value-added taxes, taxes on net worth and other form of taxation. Politicians are good at attempting to disguise tax increases. But value-added taxes will also inflate the cost of consumer goods and further increase the probability of higher inflation.

Let us now summarize our economic outlook for the foreseeable future as it will impact most of the citizens of this country. Continued high and maybe higher taxation, high and higher federal debt, reforms to the Social Security, Medicare, Medicaid and broader health care system will provide a rather bleak future economic outlook for the average citizen.

As already noted, in all likelihood we are in for slower growth, higher inflation and reforms that will impoverish to some degree not only seniors but also all Americans due to even higher taxation, higher indebtedness and slower growth. As also noted earlier, we may have long periods of stagflation.

The ultimate outcome of a greater and greater socially regulated economy is now confronting this nation. We have reached the last stages of progression noted by our alleged friend, Professor Tyler. We have become a nation of people who are highly DEPENDENT on government and who have become SUBSERVIENT (bonded) to government. At a fifty percent tax rate we are also fifty percent slaves of government.

But countries do not disappear. Yes, we are becoming a relatively poorer nation but we will continue to exist. The former Soviet Union countries continue to exist, China has instituted economic reforms and continues to exist, and Cuba too will continue to exist.

We are becoming a poorer and highly indebted nation. How long we will continue to exist as a poorer nation is dependent on our people. When people have been dependent long enough, many fear certain elements of freedom and independence. In recent trips to Russia, I spoke with people who were somewhat fearful of the risk involved in owning their own apartment instead of dwelling in government-owned apartments, which is the only way it was for many years under Communist rule. Dependence becomes a crutch for those who have been deprived of freedom. Many Americans have already become substantially dependent on government. Risk-taking becomes avoided.

How much we as a people wish to be free will have much to do with the future direction of our nation. If we remain a collective group of citizens who look to government as to when to sow and reap, we will be a nation who will seek our bread from government. If we become a nation of people who decide when to sow and reap, we will make our own bread. The issue of how much government is appropriate has long been debated but government has continued to grow. When the majority of people demand less government they will vote for those who promise less government. It is easy for people to forget that the invisible hand of Adam Smith is the hand of a free and motivated people. The iron fist of Karl Marx is the hand of dependence on government.

It is my hope that the majority of people of this nation will once again increase their desire for life, liberty and the pursuit of happiness. It is my hope that more and more people will decide for themselves when it is the proper time to sow and to reap and thereby obtain more bread on their own. It is my hope that more and more people will seek equality at a higher level than at a lower level. It is my hope that more people will appreciate the meaning of thrift and that we will not weaken the strong in our futile attempts to strengthen the weak. It is my hope that the weak will especially decide for themselves when to sow and when to reap. These are my hopes but not necessarily my expectations.

In this book we have indicated that a more complex society demands more regulations. I believe that to be true, but I also believe that the views of our founding fathers need not be abandoned in the process. Governments which govern least in a more populated, more complex and more urban society will also be governments which govern best. We need not have ever-increasing taxation, and we need not have ever-increasing amounts of debt at all levels. We need not have government administer well-intentioned and socially useful safety nets. What we need is a nation of citizens who believe in greater spiritual faith, greater courage, greater risk, and a greater love of liberty. We need more citizens who believe these are the traits that lead to the pursuit of happiness.

It is the societal and moral values envisioned by our founding fathers that made us a great and economically prosperous country. We need not abandon their principles to again become a greater nation. We have done a marvelous job in our recent history of wanting equality for all. Now we need to return to believing that our Creator endowed us with the unalienable rights to life, liberty and the pursuit of happiness. It is by our collective view of freedom and liberty that we can become a stronger and better nation.

Throughout my life, my children and grandchildren have frequently been reminded that there are no good substitutes for the following three priorities in life:

1- Love of our Creator above all else

2- Love of family, friends and neighbor as we love yourself

3- Love and embrace the values of hard work and sacrifice.

In my view these are the values that make a good citizen. These are the values embraced by our founding fathers. These are the values that make a good community. These are the values that make a great nation. These are the values that made a great nation. These are the values that can again make us a great nation.

As noted earlier, our founding fathers were not only a group of great leaders with a great vision of what government should be, but also a group of great moral philosophers. It was that great moral philosophy which helped make them great leaders.

We are indeed a nation which has been transformed. We are a nation that has not abandoned the principles on which we were founded but we are a nation that has departed too far from those principles. The principles on which we were founded led us to be a nation that provided us great economic and societal benefits.

The greatness of a nation is determined by the code of morality the people and its leaders follow. It should not be a religion-based morality as our founding fathers understood. It also cannot be a purely secular-based morality as our founding fathers also understood, because that morality has no foundation. A government without a solid faith-based moral foundation will ultimately collapse. That has been the lesson of history.

As noted earlier, our nation is in for some difficult economic times. Despite the near and intermediate term difficult economic future, this nation can again be a great nation, if it chooses a proper national morality. It is the moral fabric of a society that determines a nation's greatness. It will be the collective faith-based morality of our citizens and our leaders that can again determine a new and better direction for this nation in the future.

About the Author

George E Pfautsch spent most of his working life as a financial executive for a major forests products and paper company. His final years at Potlatch Corporation were spent as the Senior Vice-President of Finance and Chief Financial Officer. Following his retirement, he began writing and speaking about the national morality he believes was intended for this nation by the founding fathers of our country. He is the author of six previous books on the subjects of morality, justice and faith. He is the co-author of a book written by Melitta Strandberg, which is the story of her family's quest for freedom before, during, and after World War II. He is also the co-author of a book written by Leroy New, the "Guitar Wizard" of Branson, Missouri. He is married to Dodi, his wife of 50 years. He has two children and four grandchildren.